Contents

General introduction

Parents as teachers

The first years of life are a very special time – for a child and for his or her parents. More than at any other time, it is the parents who are responsible for shaping the child's world. Television, playgroup, radio, colourful books and marvellous toys bombard the young child with experiences and stimulate his or her natural curiosity. It is this curiosity that is the key to the child's approach to the world. How many times a day do we answer questions about "Why?", "What?" or "Where"? As parents, we already offer a wealth of information and experiences, so why not the basics of reading, writing and mathematics as well?

There is a great deal of positive and constructive help that parents can offer young children, based on common sense and the ideas and guidelines set out in this book. Many young children develop reading, writing and number skills successfully at home. There is no reason at all why children need to be 5+ in order to start; the intellectual leap needed is a matter of development, not age. This development can be encouraged by the games and activities described here.

One of the greatest advantages that parents can offer young children at home is time. At home, the child can be the single focus of the parents' attention. Learning that is rooted in the caring, loving framework of home can blossom. But loving care is essential. Impatience and pressure from the parent will kill the interest, enthusiasm and curiosity which are at the heart of all successful learning.

What is in this book?

This book contains a wide range of games and play-activities designed to be fun for young children. As a by-product of playing the games, the child will be picking up skills and concepts that will help the development of reading, writing and number. But it is the fun that counts! If the child seems at all bored by a particular game or activity, stop at once.

There are three sections in the book, one dealing with reading, one with writing, and one with early mathematics. Each section has an introduction giving more details about the use of the activities described. But a quick glance will show that there is a lot of material. Most children will only ever use a part of it. Don't feel that you have wasted your time if you haven't covered every activity in a given section.

Each section is divided into developmental stages. Don't push your child into going further than he or she is ready to. Stop at the first signs of 'struggle'. Leave it for a few months and try again.

Most of the activities have a "Make the game" part. On the whole, this is the parent's responsibility, but don't forget that children love to get involved in helping. As you will see, the equipment required for the games is very basic. Nearly everything can easily be found around the house, and no great artistic talent or construction skills are needed.

Jan Morrow

Head Start to Learning

JAN MORROW

Longman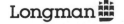

LONGMAN GROUP UK LIMITED,
Longman House,
Burnt Mill, Harlow, Essex CM20 2JE, England
and Associated Companies throughout the World

Acknowledgement:
Extract from Key Words to Literacy
by J. McNally and W. Murray
published by Schoolmaster Publishing Co. Ltd.

The illustrations are by Jan Morrow

The cartoons are by Geo Parkin

Author's note: I have used the pronoun's 'he' and 'she'
randomly throughout the book because the activities are
all equally suitable for both boys and girls.

British Library Cataloguing in Publication Data

Morrow, Jan
    A head start: an introduction to reading,
    writing and early mathematics.
    1. Education, Preschool
    I. Title
    372′.21   LB1140.2

    ISBN 0–582–00543–4

First published 1988

Set in 11/12½pt Rockwell Light, Miles 33

Printed and bound in Great Britain by
Butler & Tanner Ltd, Frome and London

Reading

Contents

Stage three: Introducing connecting words and simple sentences 33

* These are phonic activities

Stage four: The beginnings of a phonic approach to reading 46

Introduction

As parents we are aware that learning to read is very important for our children. We also realise that many children show an interest in and a love of books at an early age, and that many seem ready to read long before they are ready for school. This section of the book contains over eighty games and activities which are designed to help your child to learn to read in an informal and fun way. In addition, there is advice and information on how to approach the introduction of reading.

But before starting the games and activities, how many of the following questions can you answer yes to?

Do you make time to talk to your child?

Do you listen to your child?

Do you read to your child?

Does your child see you reading?

Does your child have his own book shelf, where colourful, well-illustrated books are available?

Do you take your child to the local library and encourage him to choose books?

Have you discovered if there are any story telling sessions at the local library?

Do you sing to your child?

Do you tell lots of nursery rhymes?

Do you use children's television programmes to stimulate conversation?

Do you provide opportunity for creative play?

Does your child communicate and play with other adults and children, perhaps at playgroup?

The more of these your child is involved in, the more useful the games and activities in this book will be.

How to use the reading games listed in this book

These games and activities should be enjoyed. Don't force your child to participate. If he prefers to play all day on his bike in the garden, so be it. Wait until the next wet day and see if he seems interested then. Keep it fun and keep the time allotted to each activity short, so that the child doesn't become bored.

The activities and games are divided into four stages and each stage should be developed before moving on to the next. Here are a few points to remember:

Don't rush through the list of games.

Keep a flexible approach and spend as much time as is necessary on each set of activities.

Move slowly and don't expect to cover all the games in each stage.

Only when you feel your child is totally confident and copes easily with the activities and games at one stage should you move on to the next.

Stage one:
Pre-reading games and activities

Stage one consists of pre-reading games and activities designed to provide a strong foundation of concepts and skills which it is necessary to develop before any "reading" can take place.

If your child doesn't go further than this stage, don't worry. He will still have acquired a depth of knowledge which will help him tremendously when he starts to read. The games at this stage are designed to help with such things as visual discrimination and comparison, training the eye to move from left to right, the development of language, the improvement of memory, and the encouragement of auditory skills through listening to everyday sounds.

Stage two:
Introducing content words

Stage three:
Introducing connecting words and simple sentences

Stages two and three contain activities and games arranged around the "look-and-say" approach to teaching reading. There are many different "methods" of teaching a child to read but basically they can be divided into three types:

Look-and-say whole word

Look-and-say whole sentence

Phonic – based on individual sounds

Variations and combinations of these three approaches are used in most schools and there are arguments for and against each of them. However, many schools start with a look-and–say approach, with phonics being introduced when the child has established a basic reading vocabulary. Stages two, three and four therefore follow this sequence.

Look-and-say

Look-and-say simply means that the child memorises and reads a whole word without first breaking the word down into letters. The child learns to read and see "cat" not "cuh-a-tuh". This allows the child to start reading simple books quickly and easily, thus building up confidence and enthusiasm for reading. Stage two uses this approach to introduce individual "content" words, such as "mummy" or "house", while stage three starts to put the content words

together with simple "connecting" words such as "and".

Phonics

Phonics are the sounds which make up a word. For example "duh-o-guh" (dog) contains three sounds. Phonics should be introduced very gradually. Most children find it very difficult to hear the individual sounds within a word since they are only used to hearing whole words, sentences and phrases. Some phonic games are included in stages one to three. (They are marked with an asterisk * in the contents list and on the page where they are described.)

The phonic games in stage two are an extension of the auditory games found in stage one. They encourage the child to "listen" to the initial sounds of words, and help him to distinguish and discriminate between sounds. At this stage, the games avoid relating sounds to letters of the alphabet. This is not to say that a child will not notice individual letters while he is "reading". Obviously he will be curious and his curiosity must be satisfied. So if he asks, simply give him the sound but not the name of the letter, e.g. "a", "buh", "cuh". Never, "ay", "bee", "see". A full list of letter sounds can be found in stage four.

Stage three phonic games do start to relate sounds to individual letters. They aim to help the child to recognise different letters of the alphabet and some of the sounds with which they are associated.

Stage four:
The beginnings of a phonic approach to reading

Stage four contains games and activities which extend the range of the phonics introduced at previous stages and lead the child to begin to break down simple words into sounds.

Stage one:
Pre-reading games and activities

Silhouette matching

Collect together:

- A sheet of paper 35cm by 30cm.
- A sheet of thick paper or card 35cm by 30cm.
- A pencil.
- A thick black felt tip pen.
- Glue and a glue brush.
- Scissors.
- A children's picture colouring book or old magazines.

Make the game

1 Look through the picture book or old magazines and find about six or seven simple pictures of familiar objects, e.g. a dog, a chair, a flower.
2 Very carefully cut round the objects you have chosen and glue them on to the sheet of card. Alternatively if you are good at drawing, draw some objects straight on to the card.

3 When the glue has dried, carefully cut round the objects and, using them as templates, draw round each one on to the sheet of paper.
4 Turn the outline drawings on the paper into black silhouettes by colouring them in with the felt tip pen.

Play the game

Ask the child to match and cover up the black silhouettes with the correct objects.

Milk-top threading

Collect together:

- Lots of clean milk bottle tops.
- A ball of wool.
- A darning needle – the type which is large and blunt ended.
- Scissors.

Play the game

Thread the needle with wool. Tie a knot at the end and thread the milk tops on to the wool. Even very young children find it easy to "sew" milk bottle tops and the finished product could be turned into a necklace.

Spot the difference

Collect together:

- *A piece of card 6cm by 6cm.*
- *A piece of paper 30cm by 15cm.*
- *Scissors.*
- *A felt tip pen.*
- *A pencil.*

Make the game

1 Take the piece of card and make a template of an animal or everyday object, e.g. a fish. If you are not very artistic, cut out a picture from a magazine, mount it on card and cut round it to make the template.
2 Use the template to draw the outline shape of the fish (or whatever you have chosen) several times on to the piece of paper.
3 As accurately as you can, draw identical details on to each fish, e.g. a fin, an eye, a tail pattern etc. Create a "difference" by missing out some of the detail on one of the fishes. The younger the child the more obvious the missing detail needs to be.

Play the game

Give the child a pencil and ask him to find the fish with something missing. He could then draw in the missing detail or simply draw a ring around the appropriate fish.

A dressing up box

Children adore dressing up. It seems to inspire imaginative play and the child has the opportunity to assume in fantasy form all sorts of different "roles". He may pretend to be a space invader, a mummy, a doctor, or any number of other exciting people. Experiencing life situations in fantasy form is not only good for children, (it can help take the fear out of strange situations), but it also helps them to understand other peoples' feelings and provides lots of opportunity for language development.

All you need to provide is a strong cardboard box full of old clothes. Jumble sales are marvellous places for buying really exotic clothes and hats which have the added advantage of only costing a few pence. It is also worth making and providing a few simple home made props such as a cloak, a cardboard sword and a few pieces of unwanted jewellery. Children also love to see themselves when they are dressed up so a long mirror would be very popular.

A scrap book

Collect together:

- *A scrap book you have bought or made. (You can make a home-made scrap book by stapling several sheets of paper together.)*
- *Paste or glue and a glue brush.*
- *An old newspaper for covering the table top.*
- *Scissors.*
- *Old magazines, catalogues, Christmas cards etc.*

Play the game

Little children adore finding interesting pictures in old magazines, cutting them out and sticking them into their very own scrap book. If cutting is too difficult they can rip the pictures out. However, some cutting should be attempted first. If your child shows any signs of being left-handed, remember that you can get special "left-handed" child's scissors from good toy-shops.

Making jigsaws

Collect together:

- *Old magazines, comics, or birthday/Christmas cards.*
- *Scissors.*
- *A piece of card the same size as the picture you choose.*
- *Glue and a glue brush.*
- *A pencil.*
- *A large envelope.*

Make the game

1 Find a colourful picture and cut it out.
2 Stick the picture on to the card and when it is dry cut it into pieces. Obviously the younger the child the fewer the pieces.

Play the game

Ask your child to put the picture back together again. When she has finished she can pop the jigsaw into the envelope to keep it safe until next time.

Colander threading

Collect together:

- *A kitchen colander.*
- *A pair of boot laces.*

Play the game

Give the child a long boot lace with a knot at one end. Ask her to thread the boot lace through the holes in the kitchen colander. If you can't obtain boot laces, use shoe laces instead.

The shopping memory game

This game is an old favourite and can be played by 2 or more players. You start the game by saying,

"I went shopping one morning and I bought a cabbage."

The next player then repeats the phrase and adds something to the shopping list, e.g.

"I went shopping one morning and I bought a cabbage and a bottle of milk."

The game continues with each player in turn adding another item to the shopping list. This is quite a difficult game, so be prepared to help little ones and don't expect them to get the shopping list in the right order.

Picture lotto

Collect together:

- *4 sheets of card 24cm by 20cm.*
- *A ruler.*
- *A pencil.*
- *Scissors.*
- *2 identical children's comics.*
- *Glue and a glue brush.*

Make the game (for two players)

1 Using the pencil and ruler divide each piece of card into 6 identical sections. Each section should be 8cm by 10cm.
2 Look through one of the children's comics and find 12 interesting and colourful pictures of comic characters. Find the same pictures in the second comic and cut out all 24 pictures. The pictures need to be small enough to fit easily into the 8cm by 10cm spaces on the cards.
3 Take the pictures from the first comic and glue them on to the marked sections on 2 of the cards. Put the cards on one side to dry.
4 Take the identical pictures from the second comic and stick them on to the sections on the remaining 2 cards. When the glue has dried cut out each section of these two cards so that you have 12 separately mounted pictures.

Play the game

Each of the two players has a complete card with six comic characters stuck on it.

Spread the loose pictures on a table top, picture-side down. Each player takes it in turn to pick a picture and try to match it with those on her card. If it is identical she places it on top of the picture on her card; if not, she returns it face down on the table. The winner is the first to cover her pictures.

Matching pairs game

Collect together:

- *12 small pieces of card, 8cm by 8cm.*
- *6 pairs of identical pictures taken from comics or magazines.*
- *Glue and a glue brush.*
- *Scissors.*

Make the game

1 Trim all the pictures so that they are just slightly smaller than the pieces of card.
2 Glue each picture on to a card.

Play the game

Spread the cards on a table top, picture-side down. Each player takes a turn at lifting two of the cards. If the pictures are the same the player can keep the cards; if they aren't, he returns them face down on the table. The winner is the one who collects the most pairs. This is a good memory game as the child needs to remember where certain cards are in order to make up a pair.

Picture story strips

Collect together:

- *A strip of card, 8cm by 30cm. This will make one story strip.*
- *A felt tip pen.*
- *A ruler.*

Make the game

1 Think of a very simple story. It doesn't have to be an elaborate tale, just a familiar sequence of events. Children love stories about themselves, so it could be something that has actually happened to your child.

2 In your mind divide the story up into not more than five sections, e.g.

A girl has packet of flower seeds.
She puts a seed in a flower pot.
She waters the seed and the sun shines.
A flower grows from the pot.

3 Using a ruler and the felt tip pen divide the strip of card into equal sections. Draw the story in pictures from left to right on to the card. It doesn't matter if you aren't particularly good at drawing. Matchstick figures would do nicely.

Play the game

Ask the child to look at the story strip with you. Point to the first picture with your finger and, as you tell the story, run your finger along the bottom of the strip.

Now ask the child to tell you the story and as she does so, guide her finger from left to right along the bottom of the card.

You can build up quite a collection of story strips. Keep them together in an empty shoe box and the child will be able to look at the stories over and over again. Children may even like to make up their own stories and draw them on to strips.

You can also cut out the sections of story, jumble them up and ask the child to put them back together again in the right order.

What's missing?

Collect together:

- *A large tray.*
- *A tea towel.*
- *A collection of small objects e.g. a toothbrush, a cup, an apple, a toy car, etc.*

Play the game

Put four objects on to the tray. Ask the child to look at them. Cover the objects up with the tea towel and while the child closes his eyes, remove one of the objects and put it behind your back.

Remove the tea towel, ask the child to open his eyes and tell you what's missing. When he guesses correctly, return the missing item and make the game a little harder by adding a 5th object to the tray. You can of course add as many or as few objects to the tray as you feel necessary.

Children also love to remove the items themselves while mummy closes her eyes and then tries to guess correctly.

Spin a nursery rhyme

The players take turns to spin the arrow. When the arrow stops spinning and points to a nursery rhyme character and number, the player must say that particular rhyme before she can move her button the appropriate number of spaces.

The buttons should be moved from left to right along the strip. The winner is the one to reach the end of the strip first.

Collect together:

- *3 pieces of card, 20cm by 20cm, 40cm by 8cm and 12cm by 2cm.*
- *A brass paper fastener.*
- *A ruler.*
- *A felt tip pen.*
- *Crayons.*
- *Scissors.*
- *A button for each player.*

Make the game

1 Draw lines to form a "Union Jack" on the 20cm by 20cm piece of card. On the outside edge of each section of the flag draw a nursery rhyme character, e.g. Humpty Dumpty, Baa Baa Black Sheep, a Twinkle Twinkle Little Star and so on. At the side of each character print a number. Ask your child to help you colour the pictures.
2 Make a spinner by cutting out an arrow from the 12cm by 2cm piece of card and attach it to the middle of the flag with the brass paper fastener. Make sure that it is loose enough to spin easily.
3 Using the ruler and pen divide the 40cm by 8cm strip of card into 20 sections.

Play the game

Each player takes a button and places it at the start of the 40cm strip.

Simple riddles

Play the game

Ask the child to answer some very simple riddles for you. Make sure the subject matter of the riddle is very familiar to the child, e.g.

Grown-up: "What's grey and warm and furry and sleeps on top of the boiler in the kitchen?"

Child: "Jessicat!"

In this example the grown up is providing and using descriptive words about a familiar object, i.e. the family cat. At the same time the child is learning to listen carefully, and she is extending in a receptive way her own vocabulary. When you feel the child has grasped the idea of the game, ask her to make up a riddle for you. At first she will find it hard not to actually name what she is thinking of, but gradually she will begin to make up descriptions for herself.

Printing

Collect together:

- *Empty cotton reels, potatoes cut in half, carrot tops, corks, toy bricks, etc.*
- *Sheets of paper. (Old newspaper would do.)*
- *Ready mixed liquid paint. 2 colours are usually sufficient.*
- *A paint brush or 2 old sponges and 2 plates.*

To make a print

Provide the child with the objects, paper and paint.

If using paint and a paint brush the child simply covers one side of an object with paint and presses the painted surface on to the paper.

If using the sponges and plates, you put each sponge on to a plate and thoroughly soak the sponge with the paint. The child presses the objects on the sponge before printing on to paper.

This activity is great fun and the child should be left to enjoy herself, but if she is printing a pattern across the paper do remind her to print from left to right.

Hand puppets

Collect together:

- *A sheet of card 30cm by 20cm.*
- *Scissors.*
- *Felt tip pens or crayons.*
- *2 long cardboard tubes. The type used to hold tinfoil would be fine.*
- *Sellotape.*

Make the game

1 Ask the child to lay one of his hands with fingers outstretched on to the sheet of card. Help him to draw round his hand with the felt tip pen in order to obtain a hand outline. Do this with both hands.
2 Cut the hand outlines out and draw faces on the palms. Stick the hand people on to the top of the cardboard tubes with some sellotape.

Play the game

Encourage your child to make up stories and little plays for the hand people. Why not provide a puppet theatre by hanging a sheet between two kitchen chairs.

The washing day game

Collect together:

- *A sheet of plain paper, 20cm by 30cm.*
- *A felt tip pen.*
- *Some patterned paper.*
- *Scissors.*

Make the game

1 Draw a simple washing line on to the sheet of plain paper.
2 Draw and cut out several small items of clothing from the patterned paper, e.g. a dress, a pair of trousers, a scarf, a pair of gloves.
3 Using the cut-out clothes as templates, draw the outline of the clothes on to the washing line.

Play the game

Give the child the cut-out clothes and ask him to hang the washing out to dry by matching the cut-outs with the drawings on the line. Encourage the child the fill the washing line from left to right.

What is it?

Collect together:

- *A blackboard and chalk or a large sheet of paper and a pencil.*

Play the game

A grown-up should start to slowly draw an animal or object on to the blackboard. Ask the child to guess what the animal or object is. If the child can guess correctly before the picture is finished, she scores a point.

For an interesting variation on this theme and one which makes the game a little harder for older children the grown-up should draw the objects as seen from above.

In the bag

Collect together:

- *A pillow case.*
- *A collection of objects such as an apple, a comb, a rubber glove, etc. (Make sure that the child does not see the objects.)*

Play the game

Put the objects into the pillow case. Ask the child to dip his hand into the bag and feel round for one of the objects.

Without removing the object ask him to tell you what he can feel. If he finds this difficult ask him a few questions about it, e.g. Is it soft or hard, smooth or rough?

When he has finished describing the object and has guessed what it is, he removes it from the bag and starts again.

Alternatively, the adult could put a hand in the bag and describe one of the objects to the child. Again the child should try to guess what the object is.

*Sounds lotto 1

(To make a game for two players)

Collect together:

- *A cassette recorder and blank tape.*
- *2 sheets of card or paper 20cm by 15cm.*
- *A ruler.*
- *A felt tip pen.*
- *8 buttons.*

Make the game

1 Take the cassette recorder and tape 8 familiar sounds with a short silence between each one. The sounds could include, e.g. a tap running, the telephone ringing, the door bell ringing, the dog barking, the clock ticking, the toilet flushing, hoovering, and whisking an egg.
2 Take the sheets of card and divide each one into 4 equal sections. Draw a simple picture of one of the objects which make the sounds in each section. Make sure that you do not draw the pictures in the same order as the sounds on the tape.

Play the game

Each child takes a card and a pile of buttons and listens carefully to the tape. Each time he hears a sound, he looks at his card and if he can see a picture of the object which makes the sound he places a button on top of the appropriate picture.

The winner is the one whose card is full of buttons first. Obviously one of the cards is always going to be the "winner's" card. So before the children notice this fact, make sure that they all get a turn with that particular card. When they finally realise the game is "fixed", start again by making a new collection of pictures and/or recordings.

*Beat out rhythms

This is a clapping game. Start by clapping out the number of syllables in your child's name, e.g.

> Kate = 1 clap.
> Sophie = 2 claps.
> Nicholas = 3 claps.

Sing the names as you clap and ask the child to join in.

Now try mummy and daddy, which have 2 claps each.

This activity is far harder than you may think. Little ones often don't clap rhythmically and find it hard to sing and clap at the same time. However practice makes perfect and eventually all sorts of silly clapping songs can be made up, e.g.

"The drinks song"

(Sing to the tune of *Frere Jacques*)

Coffee (2) Coffee (2)
Coffee (2) Coffee (2)
Lemonade (3) Lemonade (3)
CoCo (2) CoCo (2) Cola (2)
CoCo (2) CoCo (2) Cola (2)
Coffee (2) Tea (1)
Coffee (2) Tea (1)

*Home-made musical instruments

Home-made musical instruments are inexpensive, easy to make and great fun to play. Use them to accompany favourite nursery rhymes and songs.

Maracas

Simply fill an empty washing up liquid bottle with dried peas.

A drum

Use a saucepan and wooden spoon.

Musical bottles

Fill 5 empty glass milk bottles with different levels of water and tap with a teaspoon. (Of course young children should always be supervised when playing with glass bottles.)

A guitar

Wrap thick rubber bands around an empty shoe box or ice cream tub. (Remove the lid first.) Create the noise by plucking the rubber bands.

A tambourine

Thread milk bottle tops on to 2 or 3 lengths of wool. Cut a large hole in the centre of a round plastic margarine lid and tie the lengths of wool to the lid.

*Stop and go!

Collect together:

- *4 or 5 items which make a noise, e.g. a whistle, a rattle, a pan and spoon.*

Play the game

To start the game use two sounds only, e.g. a whistle and a rattle. Explain to the child that when the rattle shakes, she should walk round the room and when the whistle blows she should stop and stand still.

Use the rattle and the whistle alternately for a few minutes until the child is familiar with the routine. Now introduce a third sound and a third action, e.g. a clap means hop. After a while a fourth sound can be added, e.g. a bang on the pan means jump.

Be prepared to change places with your child and let her make the noises. Incidentally this is a good game for a party.

Stage two:
Introducing content words

A "reading readiness" check list

Here is a quick check list. If you can answer "yes" to the following questions, then your child, regardless of age, is probably ready to start the gradual process of learning to read using the games and activities in this section.

Is your child fit and healthy, with no hearing or sight problems?

Is she a reasonably confident child with no great emotional worries at the moment?

Can she speak clearly and in sentences?

Can she remember and repeat nursery rhymes and very simple stories?

Can she hold a conversation with other adults and children?

Can she carry out simple instructions such as, "Please go upstairs and get some clean socks from the sock drawer"?

Can she put together simple jigsaws and other manipulative toys?

Can she cope easily with the type of games and activities described in stage one?

Is she curious about things? Does she ask questions?

Does she enjoy looking at books with you and having stories read to her?

How to prepare and use "look-and-say" cards

Cut some white cardboard into strips, 11cm by 22cm. You will also need a fairly thick, black, felt tip pen.

Probably the best word to start with is your child's own name. Write his or her name with the black pen on to one of the strips of card. Apart from the initial letter of people's names, always use lower-case letters (not capitals) but do make sure that the letters are large and clear. It sometimes makes it easier for your child to memorise the words if you make each card larger and put a picture above the word. However, the picture will need to be removed after a few days, as it is important that the child learns to recognise the shape of the word without the aid of a picture.

Show the card to the child. Slowly tell her what it says and as you do so run your finger underneath the word from left to right. Never let your finger go from right to left. If you want to read the word twice, take your finger away from the card when you reach the end of the word and put it back at the beginning.

Your child will probably want to repeat the word without any prompting. But if not, ask her to say what is on the card and help her to run her finger under the word from left to right as she does so.

Repeat the whole process of reading the card to the child and asking her to read it to you.

You should aim to read the card together several times a day during the next day or two. BUT make sure that the reading sessions are very, very short. Young children are able to concentrate for only a very limited time. Be sure that you don't interrupt the child to read to you when she is playing a favourite game or happily watching television.

After a couple of days, introduce the next look-and-say card. The word should be "mummy" or "daddy". The aim is to introduce and slowly build up a collection of "family" look-and-say words. These could include the names of sisters, brothers, family pets, best friends and so on.

As well as reading the look-and-say cards, the child should be using these words in the games and activities listed in this section. For example, as well as reading the word "mummy" from the look-and-say card the child should be:

Making the word "mummy" out of plasticine;
Tracing the word "mummy";
Making a "mummy" badge;
Using the word "mummy" in games such as lotto.

After "family" words what then? Here are some suggestions...

Home words: table, door, bed...
Favourite toy words: Lego, bike, doll...
Animal words: dog, cat, horse...
Food words: sweets, chips, apple...
Colour words: red, blue, green...
Action words: jump, run, hop...
Place words: park, shop, playgroup, garden...

All of these are examples of "content" words. As you can see, at this stage small connecting words such as "is" and "the" are not introduced. You may feel that because "is" and "the" are small in size that they must be easy to memorise, but this is not so. They are not easy words for a child to understand. You can't actually see an "is" but you can see and understand a content word such as "television". And understanding is the key to learning. The introduction of connecting words should be left until later and is covered in stage three.

Keeping a reading record

Probably the easiest method of recording your child's reading progress at this stage is to keep the look-and-say cards together in an envelope or empty shoe box. However, as children love to look at and play with their "words" it seems inevitable that some may get lost or badly stained and need replacing. Therefore, keep a note book as well which contains a list of the words your child knows.

It is important that the cards remain clean and undamaged otherwise the child may associate a particular word with a mark on the card. For example, if the card with "dog" on it is slightly torn in one corner, this may act as a visual clue to the word. The child wouldn't need to see the word "dog" he would merely respond to the tear.

Magic words

Collect together:

- *2 or 3 sheets of white paper, 21cm by 26cm.*
- *A white candle.*
- *A jar of very thin black paint.*
- *A paint brush.*

Make the game

1 Choose a word that your child is learning at the moment, e.g. dog.
2 Use the candle to draw a dog on each of the sheets of paper. Underneath each picture, use the candle again to write the word dog. You will need to press down quite firmly with the candle.

Play the game

Ask the child to discover the magic words and pictures by painting gently over the wax treated paper with the thin black paint. Small children are always amazed to see the magic words appearing.

Plasticine names

Kate

Sophie

Nicholas

Collect together

- *A sheet of card, 30cm by 20cm.*
- *Plasticine.*
- *A pencil.*

Make the game

Use one of the "content" words you are introducing to your child and write it in large (lower case) letters on to the piece of card.

Play the game

Help your child to make several long Plasticine "snakes". Help the child to use the "snakes" to make the word on the card by laying the Plasticine on top of the print. If the "snake" is a little too long or short for a particular letter you can easily add to or take away some of the Plasticine.

Do remember to encourage the child to start with the first letter of the word and as far as possible help him to form the letters correctly, e.g. If one of the letters is an "S" the child should start by placing the Plasticine at the top of the letter.

At a later stage your child may be able to make certain words such as his own name without the aid of the printed word underneath.

Family badges

Collect together:

- *Cardboard disks (one for each member of the family). The disks can be made by drawing round a small coffee cup on a sheet of cardboard.*
- *Safety pins.*
- *Sellotape.*
- *A black felt tip pen.*
- *Crayons.*
- *Scissors.*

Make the game

Make a badge by attaching a safety pin to the back of the cardboard disk with a piece of sellotape. Write the name of each member of your family on a badge. (Apart from the initial letter of each person's name, use lower-case letters.) Children also love to decorate the badges with patterns or pictures but do make sure that they don't obscure the words.

Play the game

Put the badges on and try to remember to wear them for at least two or three days. Grown-ups should point to the badges occasionally and ask the child to tell them what the word says.

Tracing

Collect together:

- *Sheets of white paper. (A good size would be 20cm by 18cm.)*
- *Greaseproof paper, cut slightly smaller than the white paper.*
- *A black felt tip pen.*
- *A pencil.*
- *Sellotape.*
- *Scissors.*
- *Crayons.*

Make the game

Initially the child should be given simple pictures to trace. When he has learnt how to hold the pencil correctly and has some degree of pencil control (see stage one of the writing section for information on pencil practice), you can provide him with tracing cards which contain some of the content words you are introducing.

1 Using large lower-case letters write some content words on the white paper with the felt tip pen (one word per sheet of paper). Appropriate pictures could also be drawn on to the paper but make sure that they do not obscure the letters.
2 Sellotape a sheet of the greaseproof paper on top of each word.

Play the game

Spend a little time looking at the tracing words with your child. Two or three tracing cards at any one time is probably sufficient. Give the child the pencil and ask him to trace the words for you. Ask him to name each word before and after he has traced it and do remember to help him to form his letters correctly. (See the letter chart in stage two of the writing section for details of letter formation.) During the early stages of writing it is advisable to sit with your child in order to encourage correctly formed letters.

If you have drawn some pictures the child can now colour them in.

Place cards

Collect together:

- *Strips of card, 5cm by 20cm. (You will need one strip for each member of the family.)*
- *A thick felt tip pen.*

Make the game

Write the name of each member of your family on a strip of card. (Apart from the initial letter of each person's name, use lower case letters not capitals.)

Play the game

At meals times when the table is being set ask your child to use the name cards to show where each member of the family is to sit. The cards can either be put on the chairs or placed in between the knives and forks.

Labelling

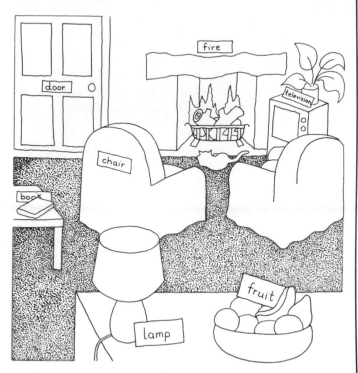

Collect together:

- *Strips of white card, 20cm by 6cm.*
- *A thick black felt tip pen.*
- *Sellotape.*

Play the game

Putting labels on to selected items found around the home is a good way of ensuring that the child sees the connection between the written word and the object it represents.

For example:

When introducing "home words", you could write the words, television, table, chair, door etc. on to pieces of card and then sellotape them on to the objects concerned.

When using "colour words" (introduce one colour at a time) you could give the child a handful of "red" cards and then ask him to go round the house and put red labels on anything red he can find.

You could also label his favourite toys and put his name on his bedroom door.

A general interest table where all the items are labelled is also a good idea. The table could contain natural objects such as stones, twigs, moss and flowers. Or it could have a theme such as "farm animals" or "things which shine".

The child's own creative work, paintings and models etc. can also be attractively displayed and labelled.

The take-a-word game

Collect together:

- *Several small pieces of card, 10cm by 6cm. (To make the game worthwhile you will need at least 5 cards.)*
- *A black felt tip pen.*

Make the game

1 On one side of each of the pieces of card write a content word that you are introducing at the moment. Remember to use lower-case letters.
2 On the other side of the cards write out some simple instructions or questions, e.g.

Jump up and down 10 times.
Who had to get home by 12 o'clock?
Run to your bedroom and back.

Play the game

Place the cards word side up at one end of the room and stand with your child as far away from them as possible. Name one of the words and ask your child to run to the cards and bring it back for you. If he returns with the correct word he should then carry out the instruction or answer the question contained on the back of the card. If he does this correctly he scores a point and keeps the card. If the child returns with the wrong card ask him to take it back and try again. (A little help may be necessary to begin with.)

This is a super game for boisterous children.

Word lotto

(To make a game for two players)

Collect together:

- *2 pieces of white card, 24cm by 12cm.*
- *12 small pieces of card, 8cm by 6cm.*
- *A felt tip pen.*
- *A ruler.*

Make the game

1 Use the ruler and the pen to divide the two large cards into 6 equal sections. Each section should be 8cm by 6cm.
2 In each section write out one of the content words you are introducing at the moment. You will need 12 words altogether and these should be a mixture of words which the child already knows and some words which are new to him. If you feel picture clues may help your child to recognise the words, these should also be drawn on to the sections of card.
3 Write the words out for a second time on to the individual squares of card but this time don't draw any pictures.

Play the game

Each player takes one of the large cards and the smaller cards are turned face downwards on to the table.

The first player picks up a small card and reads the word out loud. If he finds that this small word card matches a word on his big card then he puts it on top of the word. If it does not match, then the player replaces the card face downwards on the table and the next player takes a turn. The first player to cover up all the words on the big card is the winner.

Word pairs

Collect together:

- *12 small pieces of card, 7cm by 7cm.*
- *A felt tip pen.*

Make the game

1 Decide on 6 content words, e.g. mummy, daddy, dog, Nick, Kate, Sophie.
2 Write each word on to two of the pieces of card, so that you have two cards with "mummy" on, two with "daddy" on and so on.
3 If you feel it is necessary you could also draw some pictures of mummy, daddy, etc. just above the printed words. However, if you do this, you will need larger pieces of card.

Play the game

Place the cards word side down on to the table or floor. The child picks up one card and says the word. He then picks up another card and says the word. If the two words are the same he can keep them. If not he puts them back face downwards on to the table.

The next player now has a turn. The winner is the one who finds the most pairs. This is a good reading activity and the child also has to "remember" where to find a pair.

Win the word

(To make a game for two players)

Collect together:

- *10 pieces of stiff white paper or card, 15cm by 5cm.*
- *A felt tip pen.*
- *2 sentence racks. Detailed instructions for making the racks can be found in stage three.*
- *A ruler.*

Make the game

1 Choose 10 content words. Write each word on one of the cards, placing the words exactly 7cm from the bottom of each card. Draw a simple picture above each word.
2 On the back of the cards, write out the words again. Place the words 7cm from the bottom of each card but this time, don't draw a picture.

Play the game

Two players sit opposite each other.

Each player takes 5 of the cards and puts them in the cardboard sentence rack so that he can see the words and pictures but his opponent can see only the words.

Both players place their hands behind their backs.

The first player asks, "Where have I hidden the . . .

cat?" Both players quickly point to the "cat" card and the one who gets there first keeps the card.

Hands are again put behind backs and the winner then asks, "Where have I hidden the . . . ball?"

The overall winner is the one with the most cards.

Word skittles

Collect together:

- *Large, empty washing-up liquid bottles. You will need at least five.*
- *Sellotape.*
- *A few sheets of paper, 30cm by 22cm. (You need as many sheets of paper as there are bottles.)*
- *Scissors.*
- *A felt tip pen.*
- *A ball.*

Make the game

1 Wrap a sheet of paper round the middle of each bottle and sellotape it into position.
2 Using large clear lower-case letters write a content word onto the front of each bottle.

Play the game

Stand the bottles up in a group and ask the child to see how many skittles he can knock down with the ball. He scores a point for every bottle he knocks down, providing he can say the word on the bottle.

Word snap

(To make a game for two players)

Collect together:

- *20 cards, cut out from either stiff paper or white card. The cards should be 8cm by 8cm.*
- *A black felt tip pen.*

Make the game

Write out 10 content words on the cards. (Each word should be written on 2 cards.) Be sure to make your letters large and clear. Always use lower-case letters and try to make the words a uniform size.

Play the game

The players should sit next to each other so that they can each see the words the right way up. To begin each player takes 10 cards and holds them in his hands, they then take turns at placing the cards on top of each other on the table top. When a player sees two words which are the same, instead of calling out the usual "snap" he calls out the word and wins the pile of cards. The winner is the one with the most words in his hands.

What am I?

Collect together:

- *10 pieces of blank card, 6cm by 6cm.*
- *A felt tip pen.*

Make the game

Write the names of ten different animals on the pieces of card. Shuffle the cards and lay them face downwards on the floor.

Play the game

Take turns to pick up a card, and without showing the word to anyone else, mime the "animal word". The audience has to guess what the word is, and the person who guesses correctly picks up the next card. As well as animal words you could use action words such as run, jump, skip and hop, or family words such as mummy, daddy, etc.

Simple recipe cards

Collect together:

- *A sheet of paper or card, 15cm by 35cm.*
- *Felt tip pens.*
- *A ruler.*
- *The ingredients and utensils needed for your recipe.*

Make the game

Using symbols, numbers and a limited number of appropriate words, make a simple recipe card for your child to use.

As you can see from the illustrated "Cheese scone recipe card" very few words are used and children soon become adept at interpreting the illustrations and symbols. However, do make sure the recipe you select is as simple as possible and always set out the instructions on the card from left to right.

Play the game

Provide the child with the recipe card, necessary equipment and ingredients. Be on hand to help interpret the card and to put the scones into and out of the oven.

Word donkey

(To make a game for two players)

Collect together:

- *20 pieces of card, 14cm by 5cm.*
- *2 sentence racks. Instructions for making the racks can be found in stage three.*
- *A felt tip pen.*

Make the game

1 Decide on 10 content words.
2 Write each content word on two cards. The words should be 7cm up from the bottom of each card. Draw a simple picture above the words.
3 On the back of each card write out the words again but this time don't draw a picture.

Play the game

The two players sit opposite each other. Each player has a sentence rack. One of the cards is removed from the pack and the remaining cards are divided between the two players. The players then look through their cards and put on one side any matching pairs of cards they find.

The remaining cards are put in the sentence racks so that the player can see his pictures but his opponent sees only the word on the back.

The players then take turns to point to a word they think they need saying, "Please may I have the word . . . car." If they identify the word correctly they make take the card and put on one side any pairs they make. The loser is the person left with the odd card.

Shopping lists

The next time you go shopping for a few groceries ask your child to help you make a shopping list. Use a large sheet of paper and down one half of the paper write out the names of the items you need. Remember to use lower-case letters and make sure the words are large and clear. As you write out each word tell your child what it is and ask her to repeat the word. Ask your child to draw a little picture of each item next to the appropriate word, or alternatively you could draw the pictures and she could colour them in.

When you go shopping take a pencil with you. As each item is placed in the shopping basket, ask your child to place a tick against the correct word on the list. The pictures should help her to remember the words.

A pretend shop

Decide on what sort of shop your child would like to have . . . a grocery shop, a shoe shop, a clothes shop or perhaps a toy shop?

When you have decided, collect together as many appropriate items as possible and arrange them on a table top. If you have a toy cash register put this in the shop, but if you haven't, an empty box will do just as well. Children love to handle real money, so if you can, give them a handful of loose change. Failing this try giving them buttons or clean milk bottle tops to use as pretend money.

On some large pieces of card, write out the names of some of the items in the shop. Use large, clear, lower-case letters and remember to put the price of the item underneath the word. On two more pieces of card, write out the words "open" and "closed". Together with your child put the labels on the items in the shop. You will also need a shopping bag and a purse.

Start to play the "shopping" game. Whenever possible point to and name the words on the table top but don't be too pedantic about this; you don't want to spoil imaginative play. Use the "open" and "closed" notices and take turns at being shop-keeper and customer.

Word snakes and ladders

Collect together:

- *A snakes and ladders board.*
- *A pack of 20, 6cm by 6cm blank cards.*
- *A felt tip pen.*
- *Some counters or buttons.*

Make the game

Write a content word on each of the 20 cards. You may use the same word several times if you like and you may need to add simple pictures to help your child recognise the words. Add a number (from 1 to 5) on the corner of each card.

Play the game

When playing snakes and ladders, use the pack of cards instead of a dice. Shuffle the cards and lay the pack face downwards on the table. Each player draws the top card from the pack and the number on the card indicates his next move. The child should attempt to read the word before moving his counter.

Colour lotto

(To make a game for two players)

Collect together:

- *2 large pieces of card, 30cm by 20cm.*
- *24 small pieces of card, 5cm by 10cm.*
- *A ruler.*
- *A felt tip pen.*
- *Crayons.*

Make the game

1 With the pen and ruler, divide each of the large cards into 12 equal sections. Each section should be 5cm by 10cm.
2 In each section draw an animal or object you would associate with a particular colour, e.g. a red apple, a white snowman, a black cat, etc. Colour the pictures in.
3 On the small pieces of card write the names of the colours you have used. Remember to use lower-case letters and, if it would help your child, you could put a small dot of the appropriate colour next to the word.

Play the game

Place the small cards word-side downwards on the table top. Each player takes it in turn to pick up a word card. If the player finds that the colour word corresponds to a colour picture on his large card he puts the word on top of the picture. If the word doesn't match any of his pictures, he replaces the word face downwards on the table. The first player to cover all his pictures is the winner.

Colour by words

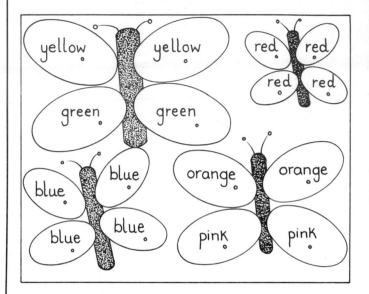

Collect together:

- *A sheet of paper, 25cm by 20cm.*
- *A felt tip pen.*
- *Crayons.*

Make the game

1 Draw a very simple picture on to the sheet of paper, e.g. a butterfly.
2 Write some colour words, e.g. red, blue, green, on the different sections of the butterfly's wings.

Play the game

Give the child the picture and some crayons. Ask her to colour in the butterfly's wings using the correct colours. If the words are new to the child, it might help if you put a small dot of the appropriate colour next to each colour word.

Jump! Skip! Hop!

Your child picks up the first card, e.g. jump. He then jumps to the next card and continues to read and carry out the instructions until he has completed the course.

Number word sorting

Collect together:

- *7 pieces of 20cm by 8cm card.*
- *A felt tip pen.*

Make the game

Write some action words on the blank cards, e.g. jump, run, walk, hop, skip, crawl, roll.

Play the game

There are two versions of this game; you can play it either indoors or out.

The indoor version

Clear as large a space as possible in the centre of the room. The adult should hold up one card at a time and ask the child to read the card and carry out the action. If the child does this successfully, he keeps the card. The aim of the game is for the child to win all the cards. Obviously adults should also take a turn at carrying out the action words.

The outdoor version

You will need a large grassy area. Lay the cards at intervals either in a long line or, if space won't permit this, around the perimeter of your lawn.

Collect together:

- *A bun tin with a dozen sections.*
- *A handful of assorted dried peas, rice and beans. (Don't use dried red kidney beans as these are dangerous if swallowed.)*
- *12 small pieces of paper, 3cm by 2cm.*
- *A felt tip pen.*
- *Sellotape.*

Make the game

Write some number words, e.g. one, two, three, etc., on the small pieces of paper and sellotape the words inside the sections in the bun tin.

Play the game

Give the child the dried peas and beans. Ask him to read the different numbers and to place the correct number of peas in each section. You will of course need to give your child quite a lot of help at first as he will not only be coping with new words but he will also be dealing with the concept of number.

Colour labels

Collect together:

- *16 pieces of 10cm by 5cm card.*
- *8 different coloured pencil crayons, e.g. black, red, blue, green, yellow, pink, orange, brown.*

Make the game

Take the blank cards and write various colour words on them using the appropriately coloured pencil crayons.

Play the game

Give the child the cards and ask him to look around the house and label colourful items with the correct colour word, e.g. he could put a "blue" label on his bedspread and a "green" label on a bowl full of apples.

At a later stage you could make a second set of cards using a black felt tip pen, which of course wouldn't provide a colour clue to the word.

* A sounds bag

Collect together:

- *An old pillowcase.*
- *A collection of objects, e.g. an apple, a fork, a pencil, a toy car, etc.*

Play the game

Put one of the objects (e.g. an apple) into the pillowcase without the child seeing what it is. Ask the child to put her hand in the bag and feel for the object. Tell her that the object starts with the sound "a", and ask her if she can tell you what the object is. If she guesses correctly, take the apple out and put something else in the bag.

Later, when the child is a little more sure of her initial letter sounds, you can ask her to tell you what sound the object in the bag starts with.

* A sounds table

Together with your child, decide on a sound, e.g. "b". Look around your home and collect together any objects which start with the initial sound . . . b, e.g. ball, banana, bat, brush, book, a brown belt. Arrange the objects on a table top and label them.

* I spy sounds

Play the game

If you have a couple of minutes to waste, e.g. while waiting in the doctor's waiting room or while peeling the potatoes, the traditional game of I spy is a valuable game to play with your child. Do remember to use the sound and not the name of the initial letter and it also helps little children if you also give a clue, e.g. "I spy with my little eye something on my face beginning with . . . n . . ."

Stage three:
Introducing connecting words

Putting words together

By this stage your child should be able to "look-and-say" quite a number of separate "content" words, e.g. mummy, daddy. You can now begin to use "connecting words" (e.g. "and" "the") to string the "content" words together to form simple phrases, e.g. "mummy and daddy".

The decision as to which connecting words to introduce first has been simplified for us by the work of J. McNally and W. Murray, who have drawn up a "key words" list. Although most adults know about 20,000 different words, McNally and Murray have shown that the following 12 words make up a quarter of what we read and write.

a, and, he, I, is, in, of, it, the, that, was, to.

McNally and Murray's key words list (part of which is reproduced in this section) shows that these 12 words plus a further 20 words make up a third of all we read. It would therefore be sensible when introducing "connecting" words to choose words from the key words list. Indeed many published reading schemes for children do just that.

How to introduce "connecting" words . . .

To put the word "and" on a look-and-say card and ask the child to learn it out of context is pointless since it will have no meaning. Therefore dispense with the look-and-say cards at this stage and concentrate on using your chosen "connecting" words in the games and activities described in this section.

A key word list

The words are grouped in order of written frequency. The first 32 words make up a third of all you read.

a, and, he, I, in, is, it, of, that, the, to, was.

all, as, at, be, but, are, for, had, have, him, his, not, on, one, said, so, they, we, with, you.

about, an, back, been, before, big, by, call, came, can, come, could, did, do, down, first, from, get, go, has, her, here, if, into, just, like, little, book, made, make, me, more, much, must, my, no, new, now, off, only, or, our, other, out, over, right, see, she, some, their, them, then, there, this, two, when, up, want, well, went, were, what, where, which, who, will, your.

A treasure hunt

Collect together

- *Several sheets of paper.*
- *A felt tip pen.*
- *Treasure, e.g. an apple, a biscuit or a 5p coin.*

Play the game

The aim of the game is to give the child simple written clues which she will follow in order to find the treasure. For example on the first sheet of paper you could write "look in the kitchen". In the kitchen the child would find a second sheet of paper saying "look on the television" and so on. Eventually after following all the written instructions the child finds the treasure. This game is great fun for energetic children especially if some of the clues are out in the garden.

A child's own word file

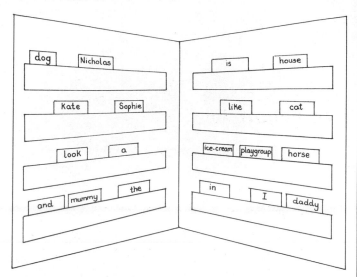

Collect together:

- A sheet of card, 44cm by 32cm.
- 8 strips of card, 20cm by 3cm.
- Sellotape.
- Small rectangles of card, 6cm by 3cm.
- A felt tip pen.

To make the file

Fold the large sheet of card in half to make a folder. Inside the folder turn the strips of card into long pockets by sellotaping each strip down on three sides. Make sure that the strips are not too close together. You should be able to get 4 strips on each half of the folder.

On the top half of each of the little rectangles of card print a word that your child can read or one that you are introducing at the moment.

Slip the little word cards into the pockets in the folder so that the words can be seen.

Using the word file

Your child now has instant access to his words and new words can easily be added to the collection. The words from this file can also be used with the "sentence rack" to make simple sentences.

A sentence rack

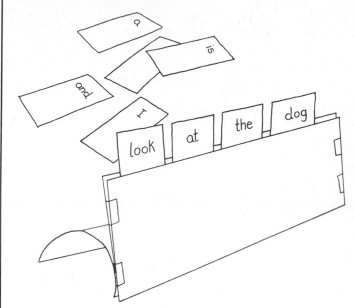

Collect together:

- A piece of card, 10cm by 25cm.
- Sellotape.
- A long cardboard tube. The tube needs to be 25cm long.
- Scissors.

Make the rack by:

1 Cutting the cardboard tube in half along its length. Keep one half and discard the other.
2 Fold the piece of card in half along its length and stick the ends together with sellotape so that you have a double thickness of card.
3 Lay the tube cut side down on a table top and sellotape the folded cardboard on to it, making sure that the "open" side of the folded cardboard strip is uppermost. The tube prevents the card from falling over.

Using the sentence rack

The child can now stand the little word cards (taken from his own word file) in the sentence rack to form simple sentences. The rack is also used in various word games found in this book.

Word bricks

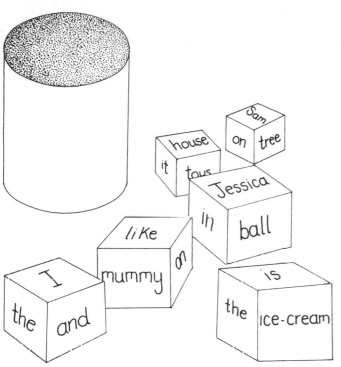

Collect together

- *6 children's wooden bricks.*
- *A black felt tip pen.*
- *Some counters or buttons.*
- *An empty tin.*

Make the game

Write some of the words your child has learnt on to the bricks. One word for each side of the cube. For every "content" word e.g. "dog", write two "connecting words". Obviously you can repeat common ones such as "and", "is", and "the".

Play the game

Put the bricks in a tin, give the tin a good shake and tip the bricks out. Can the child make a sentence from any of the top words on the bricks? If he can, he scores a point and takes a counter. If not, he puts the bricks back in the tin and the next player takes a turn.

Build a sentence game

Collect together:

- *A few sheets of paper.*
- *A felt tip pen.*
- *Several small pieces of card, 5cm by 5cm. The exact number of cards will rather depend upon the number of words used in the sentences.*
- *A pencil.*

Make the game

1 Using a few words from the "key words list" and the content words your child has learnt, write out two or three simple sentences on the individual sheets of paper, e.g.

Kate and Sophie are in the garden.
Nicky is in the house.
Toby and Jessica are playing ball.

2 Write all the words from the sentences on to the individual pieces of card.

Play the game

Each player is given a sheet of sentences to look at. Read through the sentences together so that the child is familiar with all the words. Place the individual word cards face downwards in the centre of the table.

The first player lifts a word card and if it corresponds to the first word in any of his sentences he keeps the card, places it on the table in front of him and, using the pencil, crosses the word off his sheet of sentences. The next player then takes a turn.

The aim of the game is for the child to build up a complete sentence from the individual cards, using the sentences on the paper as a reference.

If a player lifts a card and it is not the next word in any of his sentences he returns the card face downwards on the table top. The winner is the one who completes all his sentences first.

The missing word game

Collect together:

- *A few sheets of paper, 30cm by 25cm. You will need one sheet of paper for each player.*
- *A felt tip pen.*
- *Several small pieces of card, 5cm by 3cm. The exact number of cards will rather depend on the number of missing words you use in the sentences.*

Make the game

1 On each of the large sheets of paper write two or three simple sentences but miss out one word from each sentence. (The words in the sentences should be taken from the key word list, and also from the child's content word list.) The space where the missing word should be, needs to be 6cm long.
2 Write out the missing words on to the individual small cards.

Play the game

To begin with, help the child to place the missing words in the sentences and read the sentences together.

Remove the small cards, shuffle them and put them in a pile in the centre of the table. Each player takes a turn at lifting a card and if the word is one of his missing ones he places it in his sentence. If it isn't a word he needs he puts it back at the bottom of the pile.

The winner is the one who completes all his sentences first.

A letter in the post

Children love to receive a real letter in the post. The letter can be from Father Christmas (even during the summer months children like to hear from Santa), from a pet, from Gran, or simply from you. When writing the letter remember to keep the sentences short and simple and use lots of familiar content words. Little illustrations can help the child remember words, as well as making the letter more interesting to look at.

When the postman has been, read the letter together. As you read, run your finger underneath each word, this helps to train the childs eye to scan from left to right. If you wish, you could help your child to write a simple reply, but do remember to use lower-case letters.

Sentence and picture matching

Collect together:

- *5 pieces of 20cm by 5cm card.*
- *5 pieces of 10cm by 10cm card.*
- *A felt tip pen.*
- *Crayons.*

Make the game

1 On each of the 20cm by 5cm pieces of card, write a simple sentence using the content words your child already knows and a limited number of connecting words taken from the key words list, e.g.

   I like the dog.
   I like mummy and daddy.
   I like ice-cream.

2 On the square cards draw a simple picture to illustrate each sentence. Your child might like to colour the pictures in.

Play the game

Together with your child read the sentences and look at the pictures. When your child seems confident with the new words ask him to match each picture with the appropriate sentence.

Capital letter snap

(To make a game for two players)

Collect together:

- *34 pieces of 8cm by 8cm card.*
- *A felt tip pen.*

Make the game

1 On twelve of the small cards write some of the words your child knows well, (one word per card). Don't use first names as these should have already been given an initial capital letter. Write the words out using lower-case letters.

2 Write the words out again on the remaining twelve cards but this time start each word with a capital letter.

Play the game

Shuffle the cards and divide them between the two players. The cards can be used to play the traditional game of snap but instead of calling out "snap" the child calls out the word to win the cards.

A sentence race game

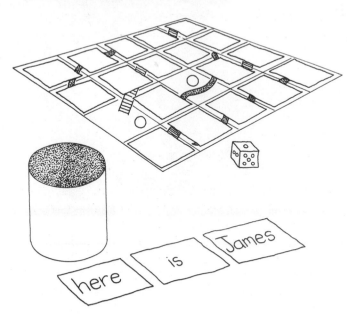

Collect together:

- *The base board from a game such as snakes and ladders or ludo.*
- *Small pieces of card. (You will need as many as there are squares on the board and they will also need to be the same size as the squares on the base board.)*
- *A dice.*
- *A felt tip pen.*
- *A counter for each player.*

Make the game

1. On the small squares of card write out some of the content words your child already knows and some of the connecting words taken from the key words list. Obviously with so many cards to fill you will need to repeat some of the words.
2. Place the cards, word side up, on each of the squares on the base board.

Play the game

Each player takes turns at throwing the dice to determine how many spaces he moves. When a player lands on a square, he removes the word and keeps it safe. When he has sufficient words he tries to make a sentence with them. If he succeeds in making a sentence he may move his counter an extra space for each of the words in the sentence. After a sentence has been made the words are returned to the board on any vacant square.

The winner is the one to reach the end of the base board first.

Home made reading books

Home made reading books are inexpensive to make.

They appeal to the child because the content can reflect her interests.

They introduce new words at the child's own individual pace.

Because the child has been actively involved in the production of the book, her motivation to read the book is high.

To make the book, either buy a plain sketch book or staple together sheets of white paper. Involve the child by first of all ascertaining what sort of book she would like to read, e.g. a fairy story, a football story or perhaps a story about one of her favourite toys.

Whatever type of book you decide on it should have plenty of pictures in it. These can be drawn by the child herself, or she could cut out photographs and stick them into the book. Be sure to leave enough space for the text.

The text should again be a joint effort between yourself and the child, but do remember to keep the sentences as simple as possible. Ask the child what she would like to say about each picture and then write down a simplified version underneath the illustration. The adult should write in the text, using large, clear lower-case letters. Ask the child to watch you while you write and say each word out loud as you write it.

One cannot over-emphasise the importance and impact of such books. As the child has been actively involved in the production of the book and as the sentences will be in essence her words, she should have little difficult in reading the book with you. This in turn will give her plenty of reading confidence, which will benefit her greatly when she approaches published reading matter.

A weather calendar

Collect together:

- *A large sheet of cardboard, 30cm by 30cm.*
- *13 strips of 20cm by 7cm card.*
- *4 strips of 9cm by 2cm card.*
- *A felt tip pen.*
- *Sellotape.*
- *A pencil and a few crayons.*

Make the game

1 At the top of the very large sheet of card write the words "Today is". Underneath the writing place two of the 9cm by 2cm strips of card. The strips need to be put in a vertical position about 16cm apart. Stick a little sellotape at the top and bottom of each strip so that they stay in position.
2 Just below the strips write the words "It is" and beneath the writing sellotape the remaining two 9cm by 2cm strips in a vertical position, 16cm apart.
3 On seven of the 20cm by 7cm strips of card write the names of the days of the week. Use lower-case letters and print the words in the centre of each strip of card.
4 On the remaining six 20cm by 7cm strips of card write the words, sunny, raining, windy, cloudy, foggy and snowing. On the back of each of these cards ask your child to draw a picture of the weather. For example, on the "windy" card he might like to draw a kite flying.

Play the game

To use the weather calendar, your child must first find the card with the correct day of the week printed on it. This is then slipped through the first set of strips beneath the words "Today is". Your child will obviously need a little help in finding the word at first.

Finding the correct weather picture can be turned into a game if you turn the cards picture side down and ask your child to read the weather words in order to find the picture he requires. When found, the card is slipped through the second set of strips under the words "It is". You can of course display either the weather word or the weather picture.

An interest scrap-book

If your child has a particular interest or hobby she may like to make an "interest scrap-book". For example, if she has a pet and likes animals, her scrap book could contain photographs, drawings, postcards and leaflets which feature domestic pets.

Talk to your child about some of the photographs and ask her if she would like to include a few simple sentences in the scrap-book. (These should be written by the adult in large, clear, lower-case letters.) Let the child decide which pictures should have writing underneath and what should be written, although you might find you will need to simplify the child's sentences a little.

A diary chart

Collect together:

- *A sheet of card 30cm by 30cm.*
- *4 strips of 8cm by 2cm card.*
- *14 strips of 7cm by 25cm card.*
- *A felt tip pen.*
- *Sellotape.*

Make the game

1 At the top of the large sheet of card write the words "Today is". Just beneath the words sellotape two of the small 8cm by 2cm strips of card. The strips need to be placed in a vertical position, 20cm apart and the Sellotape should only be applied to the top and bottom of each strip.
2 Beneath the sellotaped strips, write the words "I am" and below this sellotape the two remaining 8cm by 2cm cards, in a vertical position and 20cm apart.
3 On seven of the 7cm by 25cm cards write the names of the days of the week and use the remaining cards to describe various activities your child might regularly take part in, e.g. shopping, going to playgroup, going to the park, watching television etc.

Play the game

Hang the diary chart in a convenient place and occasionally help your child to fill in the chart by sliding the appropriate word cards underneath the sellotaped strips.

*Take-a-letter game

Collect together:

- *10 pieces of 6cm by 6cm card.*
- *A sheet of paper.*
- *A felt tip pen.*

Make the game

1 Print a lower-case letter on each of the small pieces of card.
2 On the sheet of paper make a list of the letters you have used and beside each one write an instruction or question. e.g.

a = Run upstairs and back.
b = Sing a nursery rhyme.
c = Who found a mouse under the Queen's chair?

Play the game

Place the cards letter side up at one end of the room and stand with your child and the list of instructions on the opposite side of the room. Ask your child to fetch one of the letters for you. Remember to use the sound and not the name of the letter. When the child returns with the correct letter, read out the appropriate instruction or question. If the child successfully carries out the instruction, she keeps the letter and scores a point.

A slight variation would be for the child to fetch any letter she chooses and then for her to tell you what sound the letter makes before you read out the task. If more than one child is involved they take turns at fetching the letters.

*Sandpaper letters

Collect together:

- 26 pieces of 10cm by 10cm card.
- Several sheets of heavy grade sandpaper.
- A piece of chalk.
- Scissors.
- Glue and a glue brush.

Make the game

1 Using the chalk, draw the letters of the alphabet on the front of the sandpaper. Each letter needs to be 8cm high, lower-case, and double line thickness.
2 Cut round the outline of each letter and then stick them rough side up on to the cardboard squares. (One letter per square.)

Play the game

The sense of touch is most important to young children. The use of sandpaper letters develops this sense and uses it to familiarise the child with letters and the sounds they make.

Give the child one or two letters at a time, ask him to feel the letters with his finger tips and tell him what sounds the letters make. (Remember to use the sounds not the names of letters.)

When he has explored the letters sufficiently play the blindfold game. Cover the child's eyes, give him one of the letters and ask him to tell you by touch which letter he can feel. Take turns at playing the blindfold game and if you wish to make it a little bit more competitive you could award points for each correct guess.

*Letter snap

Collect together:

- 52 pieces of 5cm by 5cm card.
- A felt tip pen.

Make the game

Write each letter of the alphabet on two of the pieces of card. Remember to use lower-case letters.

Play the game

Shuffle the cards and divide them between two players. The players should sit next to each other so that the letters can be seen the right way up. The players take turns at placing a card on to the table top. Whenever a player sees a matching pair of letters he calls out the sound of the letter and wins the cards.

*Sounds post box

Collect together:

- *5 empty shoe boxes with lids.*
- *A sharp knife or scissors for a grown-up.*
- *30 pieces of 10cm by 10cm card.*
- *A felt tip pen.*
- *Crayons or felt tip pens.*
- *Sellotape.*
- *10 pieces of 5cm by 5cm paper.*

Make the game

1 Using the scissors or sharp knife cut an 11cm by 2cm letter box opening at each end of the shoe boxes.
2 Print a lower-case letter on each of the pieces of paper and sellotape one of these into position below each letter box.
3 On the squares of card draw some simple colourful pictures of objects or animals whose names start with the letters printed on the shoe boxes, e.g. d = a picture of a dog. Alternatively you could cut out colourful pictures and stick these on to the cards.
4 Put the lids on the shoe boxes and stand them in a row on a convenient table top.

Play the game

Ask the child to post the picture post cards through the correct letter boxes. Lots of help will be needed at first, especially in discovering the initial letter sounds. You might like to print the initial letter on the back of each card.

An alternative use for the boxes would be to use the sandpaper letters described in this section and to post these through the correct boxes. Simple matching games of this type help to familiarise the child with the letter shapes.

*Letter skittles

Collect together:

- *5 or 6 empty washing up liquid bottles.*
- *5 or 6 sheets of white paper, 28cm by 22cm.*
- *Sellotape.*
- *A felt tip pen.*
- *A small ball.*

Make the game

Using the Sellotape, stick the white paper round the outside of the bottles. Print a letter on the front of each bottle, making sure that you use lower-case letters not capitals. Stand the bottles up in a group and give the ball to the child.

Play the game

See how many bottles your child can knock down with the ball. He scores a point for every bottle he knocks over, providing he can give you a word starting with the letter on the fallen bottle, e.g. "b" ... banana. Keep a tally of his and your score on a piece of paper.

Stand all the bottles up and start again. If he knocks "b" down a second time he must think of a second word beginning with "b".

*Spin-a-letter

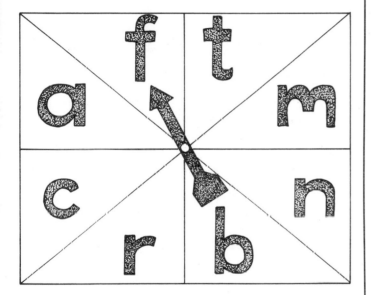

Collect together:

- *A 22cm by 22cm piece of card.*
- *A 15cm by 2cm piece of card.*
- *A felt tip pen.*
- *Scissors.*
- *A brass paper fastener.*
- *A ruler.*
- *A box of buttons or milk bottle tops.*

Make the game

1 Divide the large piece of card into eight sections by drawing a Union Jack. In each section print a lower-case letter.

2 Draw and cut out an arrow from the 15cm by 2cm piece of card. Attach the arrow to the centre of the Union Jack with the paper fastener. Do make sure that the arrow will spin.

Play the game

Players take turns at spinning the arrow. When the arrow stops spinning, the player must say out loud the sound of the letter which the arrow points to and she must think of a word which starts with the same sound.

If you like you can have a word "theme", e.g. all the words used by the players must be food names. Words must not be repeated and each player takes a button and earns a point for every correct word.

A time limit should be set for the game and at the end of that time the buttons should be counted. The winner is the one with the most buttons.

*A sounds scrap book

Collect together:

- *A scrap book.*
- *A felt tip pen.*
- *Scissors.*
- *Glue and a glue brush.*

Play the game

Devote a page of the scrap book to each sound. Start with "a" and work through the alphabet. Using lower-case letters print a letter at the top of every page.

Over a period of time help your child to fill the scrap book with pictures of objects which start with the appropriate sound. The pictures can be cut from old magazines, catalogues, and leaflets. Try to avoid objects which don't actually start with the "regular" letter, e.g. for the "f" page cut out a "fish" and a "fork" but not a "phone".

*Sounds lotto 2

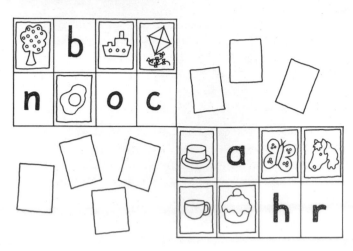

(To make a game for two players)

Collect together

- *2 pieces of 24cm by 12cm card.*
- *16 pieces of 5cm by 5cm card.*
- *A ruler.*
- *A felt tip pen.*
- *Crayons or felt tip pens.*

Make the game

1 Divide each 24cm by 12cm sheet of card into eight equal sections. Each section should measure 6cm by 6cm.
2 Decide on 16 letters you wish to introduce, and write these out in the sections on the large cards. You may prefer to use fewer letters, in which case you simply use a letter twice. (Do remember to use lower-case letters.)
3 On the small pieces of card draw pictures of animals or objects whose names start with the initial letters printed on the large cards. If you aren't particularly artistic you could cut out pictures from comics or magazines and stick them on to the cards.

Play the game

Give each player a letters card and turn the picture cards face downwards on the table. Each player takes it in turn to pick up a picture card and if the initial letter sound of the object is the same as a letter on his card, he places the picture on top of the letter. If the picture doesn't match with any of the letters on his card the player returns the picture face downwards on the table and the next player takes his turn.

The winner is the first one to cover up all his letters with pictures.

Please note, lots of help is needed at first to "hear" the initial sound in a name. A grown-up should slowly say the name of the object or animal to the child, with the emphasis on the initial letter sound.

How to choose and use a reading book

Listening to your child read is one of the most productive, educationally valuable activities you can provide. Children who read regularly to their parents improve their reading skills and soon move on to the second phase of being able to read alone.

Choose your child's first "reading" books on your own. Children don't realise their own limitations when first starting to read. They may well pick up and fall in love with books which are totally unreadable in terms of reading age and then you have the tricky problem of gently persuading them that a particular book is unsuitable. Of course the child should have plenty of opportunity to choose books at the local library or when spending her birthday book token.

Many large bookshops and book departments in large stores have educational sections where simple, colourful reading material can be found. Buy several books at the same time. Once your child starts to read, she will want to progress from one book to the next quite quickly and as the length of the text in these books is deliberately limited, progress tends to be rapid. It is sometimes best to opt for one particular "reading scheme" initially and to buy several graded books at the first level. The advantage of this is that such schemes introduce new words very gradually, have lots of material at the same level and repeat words frequently. It is important that the child has plenty of books to read but does not over-reach herself by being faced with too many new words at once.

What to look for in a first reading book:

1 The books should be interesting and relevant to your child. Certain schemes do feature one-parent families or ethnic children. Try to match the book with the child.
2 The book should look bright and exciting, with colourful illustrations.
3 There should be no more than ten words to a page and if it is a "first reader" considerably less, i.e. three or four.
4 The text should repeat words frequently.
5 The text should be large, clear, well laid out, and use lower-case letters.

How to use the books

Before presenting the reading book to your child, look through the book and see if there are any new words in the text which your child doesn't already know. Use these new words in some of the games and activities listed in this book. It is important in the initial stages of learning to read that your child is "successful". She must know the words in the books she is presented with. Failure or a struggle at this early stage is not to be contemplated. The aim is to provide an emotionally positive experience.

When you are sure that the child knows all the words in the book, find a time during the day when you can sit quietly without distraction and look at the book together. Look at the pictures and read the book to the child. Move your finger from left to right under the words as you read. Finally, ask her to read some of the book to you and as she reads help her to move her finger underneath the words. Remember that reading sessions should be short and frequent.

If your child seems to be "stuck" on a particular

word, wait ten seconds. This allows the child some time to think about the word. If the child still seems unable to proceed, quietly say the word for her. It's vital that the child doesn't feel she has failed to read and this can be avoided if during these initial reading experiences you foster the idea that it is a shared activity. Any word which seems to be persistently causing problems can then be practised in a few reading games.

As reading progresses, the need for learning the words prior to reading the book is greatly reduced. As the child builds up her reading vocabulary and her understanding of phonics she will be able to happily "discover" new words. A more detailed account of this process is given in stage four.

If subsequent reading books have several lines of writing to a page, a small piece of card can be used to separate the lines. The card is placed just under the line of writing your child is reading.

Your child's first reading book is a tremendously important event. It is her first step on the road to literacy. So let her know just how proud you are of her achievement. Hopefully this book will be the first of many which she will enjoy.

Stage four:
The beginnings of a phonic approach to reading

Sounds in reading

Long before a child is ready to break a word down into individual sounds, you can be helping him to "hear" the difference between sounds. The phonic activities and games in stages one, two and three were designed to encourage the child to listen to and distinguish between different sounds.

The "look-and-say" method gives a child a quick and easy start to the process of learning to read. However, by the time he has memorised and can read just over 100 words, he may well enjoy being able to discover new words for himself. He may do this by any of the following means:

A picture or the context may help him to guess the correct word. Guessing in this way is to be encouraged.

He could see a similarity between a known word and a new word, e.g. bike and like.

He may notice that some words are used as a part of bigger words, e.g. "in" . . . "into". Or he may know both "in" and "to" individually but have never put them together before.

Or he may break a word down into individual sounds.

Stage four introduces games and activities designed to help your child to break words down into their sounds and then to build words for himself by using sounds.

A sounds check list

It is important to use the regular sound of letters rather than their names, e.g. "a", "buh", "cuh", "duh", etc. By doing this you will be helping the child to hear the sounds within words, which will help tremendously when the time comes for him to discover new words by breaking them down into separate units.

Make sure that you are sounding out the letters correctly by reading aloud the following list of words. The sound that the initial letter makes is the sound to use for that particular letter.

a	a . . . pple	apple
b	b . . . ed	bed
c	c . . . at	cat
d	d . . . og	dog
e	e . . . gg	egg
f	f . . . ish	fish
g	g . . . ot	got
h	h . . . at	hat
i	i . . . ll	ill
j	j . . . ug	jug
k	k . . . ing	king
l	l . . . id	lid
m	m . . . an	man
n	n . . . ot	not
o	o . . . n	on
p	p . . . an	pan
q	qu . . . een	queen
r	r . . . at	rat
s	s . . . un	sun
sh	sh . . . op	shop
t	t . . . ip	tip
th	th . . . ink	think
th	th . . . is	this
u	u . . . p	up
v	v . . . an	van
w	w . . . et	wet
x	x does not make its regular sound as an

initial letter. You can hear the sound it makes at the ends of words, e.g. bo . . . x, mi . . . x

y	y . . . es	yes
z	z . . . oo	zoo

These are the sounds which you should practise with your child in the game and activities described in stage four.

When your child is completely confident with these regular sounds, you can gradually introduce long vowels, diphthongs and blends but this will normally be at a much later stage. N.B. The lists below give examples of these sounds. There are often many different ways of spelling each sound, but remember that it is the sound not the spelling which is important at this stage. For example, the first "long vowel" given below is "ee" as in "see"; this sound can also be spelt "ea" as in "sea". What is important is that the child learns to recognise "see" (or "sea") as the sound "s" and the sound "ee".

Long Vowels

ee . . . see
ar . . . art
or . . . order
oo . . . soon
ur . . . fur

Diphthongs (combinations of vowel sounds)

i . . . ice
a . . . ape
oy . . . toy
o . . . open
air . . . hair
ow . . . now
ear . . . hear

Blends (combinations of two consonant sounds)

bl . . . blink	br . . . brown	ch . . . church
cl . . . clear	cr . . . crown	dr . . . drink
fl . . . flower	fr . . . frog	gl . . . glue
gr . . . green	ing . . . king	pr . . . present
pl . . . play	sl . . . slip	tr . . . tree

Spot the odd sound game

Collect together:

- *20 pieces of 8cm by 8cm card.*
- *Felt tip pens.*

Make the game

1 Decide on four sounds, e.g. "h", "f", "t", "b". On the small cards, draw five pictures for each sound, e.g.

"h" . . . horse, house, hat, hen, hand.
"f" . . . fish, face, fox, finger, feather.
"t" . . . table, teapot, teeth, tomato, tiger.
"b" . . . bus, bottle, bee, boot, box.

2 On the back of each picture card print the initial sound.

Play the game

Place five of the cards all starting with the same sound, picture side up, in a row. Add a sixth card from another sound group. Ask the child to spot the picture starting with a different sound.

You will of course have to help the child at first by slowly saying the names of the objects out loud. The child can check for himself whether or not he has picked the correct picture by turning the cards over and looking at the letters printed on the back.

Sound pictures and three games

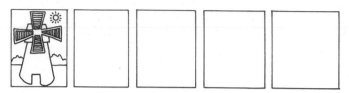

Collect together:

- *20 pieces of 8cm by 8cm card.*
- *Felt tip pens.*

Make the game

Think of ten sounds.

On the pieces of card draw some simple pictures of objects or animals which begin with sounds you have thought of. Use two cards for each initial letter, e.g.

"b" . . . Draw a picture of a bus and a bottle
"c" . . . A cup and a cat
"s" . . . A sausage and a sun
"t" . . . A teapot and a tent
"w" . . . A windmill and a window
"d" . . . A dog and a duck
"f" . . . A fish and a flower
"g" . . . A gate and a goat
"h" . . . A house and a hand
"l" . . . A ladder and a lorry

At a later stage you may like to make a second set of cards using some blends, e.g. ch . . . church and chip.

Play the games

Game one

Place the cards face downwards on a table top. The first player lifts and looks at two of the pictures and if they both start with the same sound he keeps the cards. If the initial sounds don't match, he returns the cards face downwards to the table.

The next player takes a turn.

The winner is the one who obtains the most cards.

Game two

Use the cards for a simple game of sound snap. Instead of calling out "snap" the players should call out the sound.

Game three

Give the child the cards and ask her to sort them into pairs. Each pair starting with the same sound.

Beat the clock

Collect together:

- *Several small pieces of card, 5cm by 5cm.*
- *A kitchen timer, or a watch with a second hand.*
- *A felt tip pen.*
- *2 kitchen trays.*

Make the game

1 Pick 3 or 4 words that your child knows well. Take the individual letters from these words and write them down on to the individual pieces of card.
2 Jumble the letters up on one of the two trays and put the tray at one end of the room. Put the empty tray on the opposite side of the room.

Play the game

Ask the child to stand by the tray full of letters. Start the timer going. (Use your own judgement on how long to allow for the building of each word.)

A grown-up should shout out one of the words to be made, e.g. "dog". The child has to then take the first letter of "dog", i.e. "d", run across the room and put it on the empty tray. He then returns for the next letter and so on until the word is complete. He should try to make the word before the timer buzzes!

Building word cards

(To make a game for 2 players)

Collect together:

- *2 pieces of 18cm by 12cm card.*
- *12 pieces of 5cm by 5cm card.*
- *Felt tip pens.*
- *A ruler.*

Make the game

1 Divide each of the 2 large cards into 6 equal sections by drawing two lines down and two across. Each section should be 6cm by 4cm.
2 Think of six three-letter words, e.g. dog, cat, man, hen, gun, pig. In the first sections down the left hand side of the large cards, draw a small picture of each of the three-letter objects and at the side of the picture print the initial letter of the word.

3 On the 5cm by 5cm cards print out the remaining letters from each word.

Play the game

Give each player a large card. Turn the small cards face downwards on the table. The object of the game is to build up a complete word by placing the letters in the correct order in the sections on the large card, e.g. as the first letter of dog is already on the large card, the player must find the next letter, i.e. "o". He cannot put the "g" down before the "o" is in place.

Each player takes a turn at lifting one of the small letter cards. If the letter is the one he requires he places it in the correct section. If he doesn't need that particular letter, he returns it face downwards on the table. The winner is the one to build up all three words first.

Make a word game

Collect together:

- *6 toy bricks.*
- *A black, felt tip pen.*
- *Some counters or buttons.*
- *An empty tin.*

Make the game

Print some lower-case letters on to the bricks (one sound for each side of the cube). Obviously you may like to repeat the short vowels, a, e, i, o, u several times.

Play the game

Put the bricks into the tin, give the tin a good shake and tip the bricks out. Can your child make a word using any of the top letters on the bricks? Not all the letters have to be used each time. If he can make a word, he scores a point and takes a counter. If not, he puts the bricks back and the next player takes a turn. The winner is the one with the most counters after a given length of time.

Hide and seek words

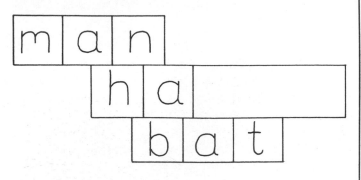

Collect together:

- *7 strips of 8cm by 20cm card.*
- *A felt tip pen.*
- *A ruler.*

Make the game

1 Use the ruler and pen to divide six of the strips of card into three equal sections. Do this on the front and back of each card.
2 Think of twelve, three letter words and then write them down on six of the strips of card. (Write one word on each side of a strip with one letter in each section.)

Play the game

Take the blank strip of card and place it over one of the word strips. Slowly slide the blank strip across the word until you have exposed the first letter. Ask the child to tell you what sound he can see.

Continue to slide the card across the strip until the next letter in the word can be seen. Ask the child to say the two sounds together, starting with the first sound. Finally expose the last letter and ask the child to say all the letters out loud again, and to say the complete word. This activity helps the child to recognise that words are built up from individual sounds.

To make the game more exciting you could ask the child to try to guess the word before all the letters have been exposed.

The name game

This is a good game for car journeys. Decide on an initial sound, e.g. "d", and a common group of objects, e.g. animals.

The first person thinks of an animal starting with "d", e.g. dog. The next player thinks of a second animal, e.g. duck. The list of animals continues to grow longer until no more "d" animals can be thought of.

Writing

Contents

Introduction

Before a child picks up a pencil and forms her first letters on paper, she should have acquired a good degree of manual pencil control and hand/eye co-ordination. We can help her to achieve such control with the introduction of some simple pre-writing games and activities.

A number of such games and activities are described in stage one of this writing section. Stage one provides lots of opportunities for pencil practice, but does not involve the use of letters. It complements the pre-reading section of this book and should be used in conjunction with the stage one pre-reading activities. (For advice on how your child should hold a pencil see stage two). At the same time, make sure that your child has plenty of access to jigsaws, paint and paper, chalk and crayons, posting boxes, building bricks and other manipulative, "Lego" type games. You may also like to obtain "chunky" crayons and pencils as these are obviously much easier for small hands to hold. Playing with Playdough and Plasticine also helps to develop hand muscles and co-ordination.

Stage two writing activities are concerned with the correct formation of letters and the writing of words. Writing goes hand in hand with reading and so the activities at this level should be used alongside those in stages two and three of the reading section.

It is also worth remembering that although reading and writing can be taught side by side, writing is in many ways a much harder skill for the child to master. Therefore her writing ability will almost certainly not be as advanced as her reading ability.

From the beginning, the correct formation of letters is vital, if the child is not to develop bad writing habits. Incorrectly formed letters will hamper her progress when she is old enough to use joined-up writing. It is just as easy for a child to learn to form a letter correctly as incorrectly; it is simply a matter of making sure that you help your child from the very first word. If you are not sure of the correct way to form some letters, study the "letter chart" in stage two.

Stage one:
Pre-writing games and activities

Shaving foam pictures

Collect together:

- 1 spray can of shaving foam. (If you haven't got any shaving foam, you can make your own by whisking together soap flakes and a little warm water.)
- 1 smooth table top or tray.

Play the game

Put a generous squirt of foam on to the table top. Now for the fun! Encourage the child to spread the foam all over the table with his hands. Make pictures in the foam by using a finger to draw with. This looks especially good on dark surfaces.

When finished with one picture or pattern the child can spread the foam and start again. It's amazing where it gets spread to – but it's very easy to clear up.

Threading

Threading is a good pre-writing activity as it encourages hand and eye co-ordination and concentration.

To begin with, your child can thread a few empty cotton reels or cardboard rings (cut from a cardboard tube) on to a long bootlace. One end of the bootlace will need to be strengthened and the best way of doing this is to sellotape a used matchstick on to the end.

At a later stage the child can use a blunt ended darning needle to thread together large buttons and clean milk bottle tops.

A wet sand tray

We have all drawn pictures in the sand at the seaside. This activity enables the child to have the same fun at home.

Fill a large shallow tray or container with damp sand and encourage the child to draw pictures in the sand with her fingers. Silver sand is preferable, as builders sand tends to stain clothes. When one picture has been completed pat the sand smooth and start again.

A salt tray

Cover a tray or shallow container with a layer of salt. Encourage your child to draw pictures in the salt with her finger. The pictures will be more noticeable if the tray is dark in colour. To remove the picture gently shake the tray and start again.

A note of caution, do make sure your child has no small cuts on her hands before she starts.

Easy sewing cards

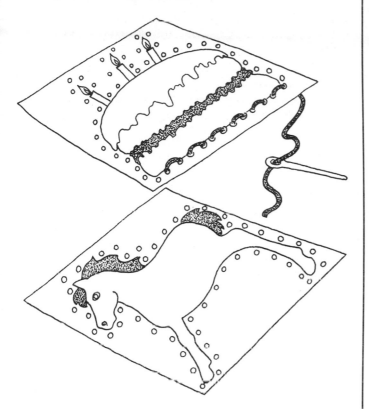

Collect together:

- *2 or 3 pieces of 15cm by 15cm thick card.*
- *A knitting needle or a pair of scissors.*
- *Wool.*
- *A large blunt-ended darning needle.*
- *A felt tip pen.*

Make the game

1 On the squares of card draw some simple, outline pictures of animals or objects.
2 Use the knitting needle or scissors to punch holes around the outside of the pictures. The holes need to be about 2cm apart. (Obviously an adult had better do this.)

Play the game

Give the child the blunt needle threaded with wool and ask him to sew around the picture by pushing the needle through the holes.

Making a blackboard

Instead of buying a blackboard which can be very expensive and rather small, why not make one? The easiest method is to buy a large tin of "blackboard paint" (available from good D.I.Y. shops) and simply paint part of an unpapered wall in your child's bedroom. The advantage of painting walls is that the blackboard area can be really large and at the right height for the child. What's more, it doesn't keep falling over! If you dislike the idea of a wall blackboard, paint as large a sheet of hardboard as you can find and stand this in your child's room. Provide lots of different coloured chalks and a duster.

Chalk is easy for small hands to hold, so children find it simple to use a blackboard. It can also provide a great deal of pleasure and enjoyment. A blackboard gives instant access to creative play and develops the imagination as it is often used in "school" games. At a later stage it can also be used for "real" writing practice.

Who caught the fish?

Collect together:

- *A sheet of paper.*
- *A felt tip pen.*
- *A pencil.*

Make the game

1 At the top of the sheet of paper draw a line of five or six pin-men figures and give each one a fishing rod. At the bottom of the paper draw a fish.
2 Draw curling, twisting, overlapping lines from the fishing rods down towards the fish but make sure that only one of the lines actually touches the fish.

Play the game

Ask the child to find out which of the figures has caught the fish by following the lines with her finger or pencil.

Templates

Collect together:

- *A large sheet of very thick card.*
- *A craft knife.*
- *Pencils and paper.*

Make the game

1 Draw the simple outlines of objects or animals on to the sheet of card. You could work to a theme, e.g. farm animals or transport. If you are not particularly artistic you could copy or trace pictures from books.
2 Using the craft knife, cut the shapes out. Obviously adults should make sure that small children don't handle such knives.

Play the game

The child can now draw round the templates on to a piece of paper. Afterwards the pictures can be coloured in.

Dot to dot

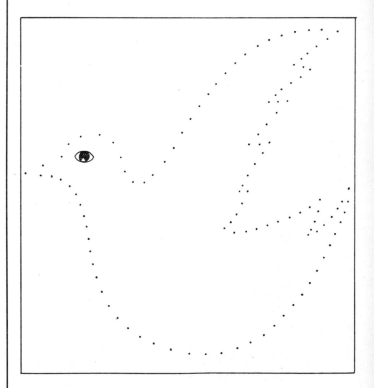

Collect together:

- *Pencils and paper.*
- *A black felt tip pen.*
- *A rubber.*

Make the game

1 Using a pencil, draw the simple outline of an animal or object on to a sheet of paper.
2 Using the felt tip pen, draw dots round the outline about 1cm apart. Rub the pencil line out and you should be left with a dotted outline.

Play the game

Ask the child to join the dots together with his pencil.

Tracing

Collect together:

- *Pencils and sheets of paper.*
- *Greaseproof paper, cut to the same size as the sheets of paper.*
- *Paper clips.*
- *A black felt tip pen.*
- *Crayons.*

Make the game

1 Use the felt tip pen to draw some simple pictures on the sheets of paper.
2 Cover each picture with a sheet of greaseproof paper and paper clip the greaseproof into position. Be sure that the paper clips don't obscure the picture.

Play the game

Ask the child to trace over the top of the picture with his pencil. He should try his best to keep the pencil on top of the felt tip pen lines. When the tracing is complete, the child can colour in his picture with the crayons.

Copy patterns

Collect together:

- *A sheet of paper.*
- *A pencil.*

Make the game

On the sheet of paper draw two or three lines of simple repeated pattern. It is best to start with a combination of straight lines and circles. Make sure that there is at least a 5cm gap between each line of pattern.

Play the game

Ask the child to copy your pattern by drawing in the gap between the lines. Make sure that he copies from left to right.

Complete the face

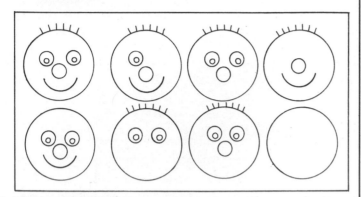

Collect together:

● *Pencils and paper.*

Make the game

Draw some large circles on to a sheet of paper. Draw a simple complete face on the first circle; this gives the child a model to look at. Leave some circles blank and give the rest an incomplete face.

Play the game

Ask the child to complete the faces with her pencil.

Follow the road

Collect together:

● *Pencils and paper.*

Make the game

Draw a long twisting road on to the sheet of paper. To make it more interesting, draw something the child likes at the end of the road, e.g. a sweetshop. Do make sure that the road isn't too narrow – 2cm wide is ideal.

Play the game

Ask the child to take the pencil and draw a line from the start of the road to the sweetshop. Ask him to keep the pencil on the road at all times.

Draw the other half

Collect together:

● *Pencils and paper.*

Make the game

Draw the simple outline shape of everyday objects but leave one half missing. For very young children draw the complete shape but make one half dotted.

Play the game

Ask the child to complete the picture or join the dots.

Mazes

Collect together:

● *Pencils and paper.*

Make the game

Draw a simple square maze on the sheet of paper. Put an arrow at the start of the maze and draw a favourite object in the centre.

Play the game

Ask the child to draw a line from the arrow to the centre of the maze without touching or crossing the lines. You could also offer a small reward, such as a Smartie or raisin, for a successful attempt.

Stage two:
Writing activities

A letter chart

Start at the star and follow the arrows

Start with the child's name

The first word most children learn to read and to write is their own name. If your child has an especially long name it is often far better to allow them to start with a shortened version, e.g. Alex instead of Alexandra.

Write your child's name in large, clear letters on a sheet of paper. The first letter should be a capital but the rest should be lower-case. Starting with the first letter of your child's name, help your child to trace over the top of the letters with her index finger. Gently guide her finger and make sure that the finger forms the letters correctly. (See the letter chart if you are unsure of the correct formation of any letters.)

As you move her finger over the letters, talk about how she is forming each one, e.g. "Let's start at the top of the 'S' and slide all the way down." Do this a few times and then give her a pencil. Always use the sound and not the name of the letter. For a list of letter sounds see the sounds check list in stage four of the reading section.

Holding the pencil correctly is obviously important. She will find it much easier if she is sitting upright at a table in a comfortable position rather than sitting on the floor. The pencil should rest in between the first finger and the thumb, supported by the middle finger. Help her to go over the top of each letter with the pencil. Encourage her to form the letters correctly and remember to talk about how she is forming them. Repeat this procedure a couple of times a day for several days, but only when the child seems enthusiastic and interested. Keep each writing session brief.

After writing directly over the top you can move on to writing over a dotted version of the name. Here the child joins dots together to form letters. Or you could place tracing paper on top of the name and ask your child to trace over it. As your child forms the letters, encourage her to say out loud the verbal instructions you rehearsed at the finger stage. Memorising the instructions in this way will ensure she forms the letters correctly when you are not guiding her.

By this time your child should be thoroughly familiar with each of the letters. You could now ask her to copy her name by writing underneath your writing. It helps tremendously if you stay by her side during the first attempts at forming independent letters. Talk her through each letter just as you did when she was tracing with her finger.

When your child seems to be confidently copying underneath your letters, give her a card with her name on and ask her to copy from the card. With sufficient practice, most children will soon memorise the order and formation of the letters in their name and will be able to dispense with the card and write independently.

This procedure of finger tracing and copying can now be applied to other familiar words. The aim is slowly to introduce to your child all the letters of the alphabet.

Fingers first

When you have a few minutes to spare, play the fingers first game. Simply ask your child to write a word he knows well in the air with his finger. Ask him to imagine his index finger is a pencil and remind him to form the letters correctly. Help him with any letters he seems unsure of, by holding his hand and gently guiding his finger.

To make the game more interesting, sit side by side with your child and ask him to write out a word or individual letter in the air while you try to guess what it is. Take turns at writing and guessing.

Word tracing cards

Collect together:

- *A felt tip pen.*
- *A pencil.*
- *Several sheets of card. (20cm by 15cm seems to be a good size for this activity.)*
- *Several sheets of tracing paper or greaseproof paper. (They need to be the same size as the card you are using.)*
- *Paper clips.*

Make the game

Using words that your child is currently learning or has already learnt to read, make up a supply of word tracing cards which can be used for tracing whenever your child has a spare five minutes.

To make the cards more interesting you could draw appropriate pictures above the words and supply the child with crayons as well as a pencil.

1 Using large, clear, lower-case letters, print out a word on each of the pieces of card and draw an appropriate picture above the word.
2 Cover the cards with the tracing paper and paper clip the paper into position. Be sure that the paper clips don't obscure the word or picture. It will help your child to remember how to form the letters correctly if you put a little dot next to the starting point of each letter.

Dot to dot words

Collect together:

- *Sheets of paper.*
- *A felt tip pen.*
- *A pencil.*
- *A rubber.*
- *A crayon.*

Make the game

1 Using the pencil, write some of the words that your child is currently learning on to the sheets of paper. Make sure that the letters are large, clear and lower-case. You could also include an appropriate picture above each word.
2 Use the felt tip pen to go over the outline of each letter and picture with small dots and then use the rubber to remove the pencil line.
3 Add a dot of colour to the starting point of each letter. This will help the child to remember how to form the letters correctly.

Play the game

Have a supply of dot to dot words and pictures available at all times so that the child can help herself to one if she feels inclined.

Cress letters

Collect together:

- *A large plate.*
- *A pencil.*
- *Blotting paper.*
- *Mustard and cress seed.*
- *Water.*

Make the game

1 Help your child to write his name or any word which he is currently learning on to the sheet of blotting paper. The letters will need to be as large as possible.
2 Lay the blotting paper on to the plate and thoroughly dampen it with water.
3 Carefully spread the seeds on to the outline of the letters. Keep the blotting paper damp and watch the cress grow into the chosen word.

Opportunities for writing

It is important that your child should see writing as a valuable means of communication and expression. This will be helped if she is involved in as many writing activities as possible, for example, help her to:

Write to gran and grandad. This is especially relevant if they live some distance away but even if they live just round the corner, writing a "real" letter and posting it can be great fun;

Write to a pen-friend;

Send an invitation to a friend to come round to play or to have tea;

Make out simple shopping lists;

Write a message in a birthday or Christmas card;

Write to Father Christmas. This is always a very popular activity!

Send a thank-you letter;

Keep a diary;

Write out some postcards while on holiday;

Label her pictures with not only her name but a title as well;

Write simple illustrated stories and poems.

No doubt you will find other types of writing that your child can do arising out of everyday activities. Encourage her as much as you can to see writing as something enjoyable and creative.

Early mathematics

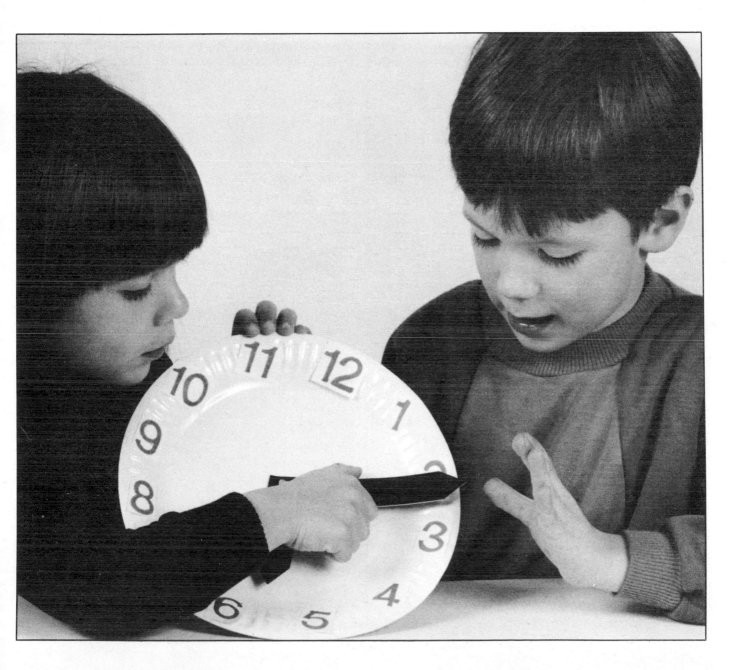

Contents

Introduction

The word "mathematics" can produce feelings of failure, confusion and even dread in some adults. Perhaps this is because an understanding of the basic concepts behind the mathematical terms has never been fully achieved.

Mathematics in schools used to be almost totally a question of learning by rote and memorising lists of numbers with no real understanding of the meaning behind the figures. Happily, "modern maths" now encourages mathematical discovery and understanding through practical activities.

The games and activities listed in this book aim to introduce the pre-school child to a whole range of basic mathematical concepts through play, discovery and enjoyment.

For example, while making a "Family hand print chart" the child is learning to understand the terms "bigger than" and "smaller than". When he plays the "Find the treasure" game, he is physically moving "backwards" and "forwards" and "counting" his steps as he does so.

The games and activities are grouped into six areas. The first area introduces some very basic number concepts, e.g. counting, matching, sorting, sharing. The first 14 games in this section use no number symbols at all, i.e. the child does not need to know and recognise the written number "5" but he does tackle the concept of "fiveness" in some detail and in very practical ways. It is important that the child should have some understanding of what "five" means before he copes with the symbol "5". The second half of this section introduces the notion of symbolic representation and helps the child to recognise the symbols that stand for numbers.

It is important that early mathematical experience should be fun. As well as the games and activities listed in this section, you should also provide plenty of opportunity for sand and water play, say lots of number rhymes with your child (e.g. One, two, three, four, five, once I caught a fish alive) and count with him at every available opportunity, for example:

Counting the stairs as you climb them at bedtime;

Counting the buttons on his coat as you fasten them;

Counting the number of sausages on his plate;

Counting the empty milk bottles as you put them out for the milkman.

It is often in the most everyday experiences that the most valuable learning can take place.

The same principle can be applied to the sections dealing with the concepts of size, colour, time, simple measurement and money. These areas can be developed in any order, and the games and activities can be chosen according to the child's interests.

Each game or activity is completely self-contained and because they are designed to be "fun", your child may well develop a liking for a particular game and may wish to repeat it several times. This is fine. Don't rush through the list of games. Take your time and enjoy playing them with your child.

As well as setting the activity up for the child and providing the materials, parents need to provide "language". It is vital that you talk about the activity or game in progress and use the appropriate words, e.g. "too many", "not enough", "the same as", etc. It is through language that the child can begin to understand the meaning of his experiences.

Number

A toys' birthday party

Collect together:

- *A small number of dolls and soft toys.*
- *A toy tea set or some old cups and saucers.*
- *An old sheet or towel.*
- *Picnic food, e.g. a handful of raisins, a few biscuits, a jam roll.*
- *A blunt knife.*
- *A few birthday candles.*

Play the game

Ask the child to arrange a picnic birthday tea for a favourite doll or teddy, and invite two or three other toys along to the party. Lay the towel or sheet on the floor and ask the child to get the picnic ready. How many plates will the toys need? This problem is easily solved if the toys are first put into position round the towel. The child can then give one plate to each toy in turn.

Give the child the food and ask him to share it between the toys so that they all get the same. Again the child will need to match one for one.

Now for the birthday cake. Decide how old teddy is and let the child stick the candles into the cake. Count the candles as they are being placed in position. (You could even light the candles and count them as you do so, though obviously the child shouldn't handle matches.)

After blowing the candles out, sing "Happy birthday" and give the child the blunt knife to cut the cake. A long jam roll makes an excellent cake for the child to cut because it is easy for him to see how many slices he has made.

If the toys aren't very hungry, the child is usually very happy to oblige and eat the picnic for them.

Spot the odd one out

Collect together:

- *Groups or "sets" of objects which have something in common, e.g.*

  Apple, pear, orange, banana = fruit
  Knife, fork, spoon = cutlery
  Jumper, socks, vest, gloves = clothing

Play the game

Place a set of objects on to a table top and include one item from one of the other sets, e.g. knife, fork, spoon, vest.

Ask your child to pick the odd one out.

You can make this game harder by collecting sets of objects whose common attributes are not as obvious, e.g.

  Plastic, wooden or metal objects.
  Soft and hard objects.
  Curved and straight objects.

Feeding the lion

Collect together:

- *An empty grocery box.*
- *A pair of scissors.*
- *A thick felt tip pen.*
- *An old newspaper.*

Make the game

1 Cut the flaps from the top of the box.
2 Draw a happy lion's face on one end of the box with the felt tip pen.
3 Crush up several sheets of newspaper to form newspaper balls.

Play the game

Pretend that the newspaper balls are the lion's dinner. Ask the child to stand a short distance away from the lion and feed him, by throwing the balls into the empty box. How many balls can he get into the lion? How many fall on the floor? The child can vary the distance between himself and the box or he could have a little competition with a friend or a grown-up to see who can get the most dinner into the hungry lion.

Tall towers

Collect together:

- *Toy building bricks.*

Play the game

Have a little competition with your child to see how tall a tower you can both build out of bricks before they fall down. Count each brick as it is placed into position and count them again when the tower has fallen over. The winner is the one with the tallest tower.

Find the treasure

Play the game

This game is similar to hunt the thimble. Ask your child to go out of the room while you hide the treasure, e.g. a chocolate biscuit. When the child returns ask him to stand in the centre of the room and guide him to the treasure by giving him instructions such as, "take three steps backwards and one step towards the window."

Make sure he doesn't go directly towards the treasure and take the opportunity to use as many different numbers and instructions as possible. As well as "backwards" and "forwards", you could also include "sideways", "over", "under" and "behind".

Setting the table

Setting the table for breakfast or lunch provides an ideal opportunity for counting and matching.

The child will first have to discover how many people he needs to set the table for and then count out the correct number of knives, forks, spoons, glasses, etc. If the child finds this rather difficult unaided, an adult could set out the correct number of chairs and ask him to put a knife and fork in front of each one.

Sorting, sets and subsets

A set is simply a number of objects which have something in common. The aim of sorting is for the child the see and classify objects into sets with a common attribute. No special equipment is needed for this. Most homes are full of objects which can be classified and sorted, for example:

If you give your child a handful of cutlery he can sort them out for you by putting all the knives together, the forks together and the spoons together;

A bowl of toy bricks can be sorted into different colours;

When putting the washing away, ask your child to help you sort it out into sets of daddy's socks, mummy's jumpers, tea towels, etc;

While unloading the shopping the child could help you to sort out the tins from the packets and the fruit from the vegetables.

As you can see there are many opportunities in a child's day to play the sorting game. Gradually introduce the term "set" at appropriate moments, e.g. "look you have made a set of forks".

At a later stage you can begin to compare the sizes of two sets by counting or matching one set against the other. You could also draw sets of objects on to paper but when you do this remember that you should always draw a ring or "boundary" around each set.

The idea of a set within a set (a sub-set), could also be introduced, e.g. "Look here are a set of farm animals (toy cows and pigs). If we put all the pigs together and all the cows together we have made two subsets."

If you provide your child with a drawn set of objects you could ask him to produce a subset by "partitioning". This simply means that he uses his pencil to separate the two (or more) different objects within the set. For example, a set of "sweets" could be partitioned into, 2 lollipops, 1 chocolate, and 2 caramels.

In real life people spend a lot of time dividing large sets into smaller subsets. When you go out to do the shopping you don't just go out to buy "food". You group certain foods together and divide the task into reasonably sized units.

Sorting into sets is a valuable experience for your child for he learns that things can be broken down into manageable groups or sets and he learns to compare, to divide and to classify according to a given set of attributes.

Copy beads

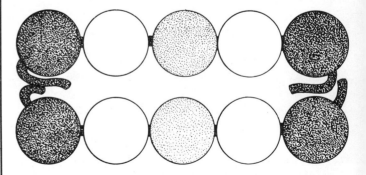

Collect together:

- *Large threading beads. If you can't obtain beads, paint some empty cotton reels different colours.*
- *2 boot laces or 2 pieces of strong string.*

Make the game

An adult should thread some beads on to one of the

laces. They should be threaded in some sort of colour and number order. Start with something simple such as, 1 red, 1 blue, 1 red, 1 blue. Later you can move on to more elaborate variations, e.g. 2 red, 3 blue, 2 green, 2 red, 3 blue, 2 green.

Play the game

Ask the child to copy your string of beads. If he manages to do this correctly, his string of beads should be identical to yours.

Square patterns

Collect together:

- *Several sheets of large-squared graph paper.*
- *Coloured crayons.*
- *Scissors.*

Make the game

1 Cut the graph paper into identically sized sheets.
2 Decide on two or three colours and colour in 5 or 6 of the squares in the centre of one of the sheets of graph paper. The squares can be coloured in any order or position but they do need to be close together. (This is quite a complicated activity, so if your child is very young, you could reduce the number of colours and squares involved.)

Play the game

Give the child the coloured square pattern, an uncoloured sheet of graph paper and some crayons.

Ask the child to make an identical pattern on her sheet of blank graph paper. To do this she will need to look at the pattern very carefully, count the number of squares and note the position of the colours.

Dressing paper dolls

Collect together:

- *A sheet of paper, 50cm by 20cm.*
- *Scissors.*
- *A packet of coloured, sticky-backed paper.*
- *A pencil.*
- *Crayons.*

Make the game

1 Fold the sheet of paper in half and then in half again. Continue to do this until you have a strip of paper 10cm wide.
2 Draw a simple doll outline on the front of the strip of paper, making sure that both the doll's outstretched arms touch the folded edge of the paper.
3 Cut the doll shape out. Unfold the paper and you will find a line of identical dolls.

Play the game

Give your child the crayons and ask him to colour a set of clothes on each doll. (Alternatively he could make some clothes from the sticky paper.) Each doll should be given a set number of items, e.g. 3, although the actual items of clothing could be different for each doll.

Spot the dog

Collect together:

- *25 cards, 10cm by 5cm.*
- *Scissors.*
- *A felt tip pen.*

Make the game

1 On one of the pieces of card draw a simple dog outline. Cut the dog out and use it as a template to draw the same dog on the remaining 24 pieces of card.
2 On each of the dogs draw some spots, i.e.

On four of the dogs draw one spot.
On four more draw two spots.
On four more draw three spots.

Continue to increase the number of spots by one each time until you reach six spots. Make sure that the dogs with the same number of spots are identical.

Play the game

The cards can be used in three ways:

to make a simple number line of dogs, i.e. the first dog would have one spot and the last in the line six spots;

as the basis of a simple matching game, by asking the child to find all the dogs with one spot etc.;

for a game of "Snap".

All about my family

Collect together:

- *A very large sheet of paper.*
- *A black felt tip pen.*
- *A pencil.*
- *Crayons.*

Make the game

1 Help the child to think about and to compare the different members of her family. She might find that there are more females than males, that everyone has blue eyes (except the dog) and that everyone but daddy likes chocolate ice-cream.
2 Some of this information can be displayed. Draw two large circles side by side on the sheet of paper and decide on which information you would like to compare, e.g. eye colour.

Play the game

In one of the circles help the child to draw the faces of all those members of the family with blue eyes (grans and grandads, aunties and uncles could be included). In the second circle draw the faces of all those family members with brown eyes.

Count up the faces in the first "set" and the faces in the second "set". Which "set" has the most faces?

Picture matching

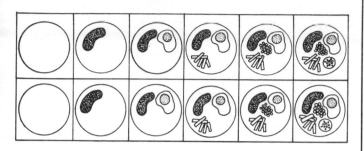

Collect together:

- *13 pieces of card, 10cm by 10cm. (One of these can be used for making templates.)*
- *Scissors.*
- *A pencil.*
- *A felt tip pen.*

Make the game

1 Decide on a theme for a picture, e.g. a dinner, a farmyard, a vase of flowers.
2 If your theme is a "dinner",

On the first two cards draw identical plates;
On the second two cards draw the plates again but this time add a fork by the side of each plate;
On the third pair of cards draw plates, forks and knives;
On the fourth pair of cards draw plates, forks, knives and a sausage.

Continue to add more detail each time until you have used up all the pairs of cards. Templates should be used when possible as they help to keep the shapes identical.

Play the game

The cards can be used in three ways:

For a simple game of snap;

The child can be asked to find the identical pairs of cards by matching one to one;

Some of the cards can be placed in a number line, with the first card showing the plate and the last card displaying the complete dinner.

Heads to hats

Collect together:

- *Sheets of paper.*
- *A pencil.*

Make the game

Down the left hand side of the paper draw a row of heads and opposite the heads draw a row of hats. You could include a variety of hats, e.g. a crown, a witch's hat, a top hat, etc. Make sure that there is a hat for every head.

Play the game

Give your child the pencil and ask him to see if each head can have a hat by drawing lines from heads to hats.

This one to one matching game could also use,

Dogs to bones
Bees to flowers
Cups to saucers
Spaceships to moons, etc.

At a later stage you can draw more heads than hats or more bees than flowers, so that the child can discover by simple matching that there are not always enough hats, flowers, bones, etc. You can then ask the question, "How many more hats do we need to draw?"

An anticipation calendar

Collect together:

- *A sheet of paper, 40cm by 15cm.*
- *A ruler.*
- *A felt tip pen.*
- *A few crayons.*

If your child is looking forward to an event, e.g. her birthday party, a trip to the seaside or gran and grandad coming to visit, you could make an anticipation calendar. This will enable your child to tick off the days leading up to the event and she can see how close she is in time to the actual day. Start your calendar a week to ten days before the event – any longer and the child will be overwhelmed by the numbers involved.

Make the game

1 Draw a ladder on the sheet of paper. (You will need to leave a 3cm space between each of the steps and you need as many spaces as there are days leading up to the event.)
2 At the top of the ladder ask your child to draw a picture of the event.
3 Starting at the bottom of the ladder write a number in each of the spaces between the steps. You need to start with the highest number first, i.e. 10, 9, 8, . . .

Play the game

Hang the calendar up on the wall but do make sure that your child can easily reach it. Each day your child can colour in one of the spaces in the ladder, starting at the bottom with the highest number and working towards the top.

Button tins

Collect together:

- *5 identical small tins with lids or 5 identical small margarine tubs with lids.*
- *15 beads or buttons.*
- *Paper.*
- *Sellotape.*
- *A felt tip pen.*

Play the game

Sit next to your child and ask her to drop one button in the first tin, two buttons in the second tin, and three buttons into a third tin.

Put the lids on the tins and rather like a magician ask the child to watch carefully while you move the tins around. Ask the child to guess which tin contains one button, two buttons and three buttons. Play this game for a little while.

Stick a piece of paper on to the top of each tin. Give your child the felt tip pen and ask her to think of any marks or pictures she could make on the paper which would help her to guess what is in the tins. Children invariably make 1 mark or scribble on the tin containing one button, 2 marks on the two button tin and 3 marks on the three button tin. Do not mention formal number symbols at this stage.

Play the guessing game again and the child will discover that the marks she has made will help her to find the correct tins. When she has become familiar with three tins you could introduce a four and a five button tin.

At a later stage the marks can be exchanged for formal number symbols.

Button cards

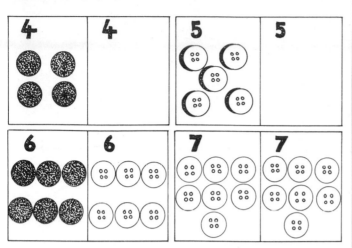

Collect together:

- *5 pieces of white card, 20cm by 13cm.*
- *A felt tip pen.*
- *A few buttons. They should be identical.*
- *A ruler.*

Make the game

1 Divide each card into two halves with a line.
2 In the top left-hand corner of the left half of the card, print a number, e.g. 3 and beneath the number draw three circles. As the circles need to be the same size as the buttons you are using, you can draw round the buttons.
3 On the right half of the card print the number 3 again. (Put it in the left hand corner, but this time don't draw any circles.)

Make several cards in this way using a different number for each one.

Play the game

Give the child a card and some buttons. (Do remind little ones never to put buttons into their mouths.)

Ask the child to look at the left half of the card first and then to put a button on top of each of the circles. As she does so, count the buttons with her. Point to the number 3 and remind her that there are three buttons on the card.

Ask the child to put three buttons underneath the number 3 on the right hand half of the card. This will of course be slightly harder as there are no circles to help her.

When she has successfully filled a couple of cards with your help, see if she can fill a card with buttons on her own.

Matching numbers and amounts

Collect together:

- *A bun tray.*
- *A collection of small objects such as buttons, small shells, pasta shapes, etc.*
- *Circles of paper, large enough to fit snugly in the bottom of each section in the bun tray.*
- *A felt tip pen.*

Make the game

Write the numbers 1 to 10 on ten of the circles of paper and place each one in the bottom of a section of the bun tray.

Play the game

Give the small objects to your child and ask her to put the correct number of buttons etc. into each compartment. The child should count out loud as she drops each button into the tray.

A number scrap book

Collect together:

- *A scrap book you have bought or made.*
- *Interesting pictures from magazines or comics.*
- *Glue and a glue brush.*
- *Scissors.*
- *A felt tip pen.*

Make the game

At the top of each page in the scrap book print out a large number. Starting with 0 and finishing with 10.

Play the game

Look through the collection of pictures and photographs and cut out any interesting objects or animals.

Sort the cut outs into "sets", e.g.

A set of car pictures
A set of dog pictures
A set of baby pictures

Use the sets of pictures to fill the scrap book. For example page 0 would of course be left blank, page 1 could have a picture of one train on it, page 2 could have two kittens on it and so on.

Home made skittles

Collect together:

- *Large, empty washing up liquid bottles.*
- *An old newspaper.*
- *Sellotape.*
- *A felt tip pen.*
- *A few sheets of paper, 30cm by 22cm. (You need as many sheets of paper as there are bottles.)*

Make the game

1 Wrap a sheet of paper round the middle of each bottle and sellotape it into position.
2 Print a number on the front of each bottle. It is best not to go above the number 5. Beneath each number draw the appropriate number of large spots.
3 Take a sheet of newspaper and crush it tightly into a ball. Do this until you have at least five balls.

Play the game

Stand the bottles up in a group and see how many can be knocked down with the newspaper balls. The child can count how many bottles she has managed to hit; or, at a later stage, she can add up the score on the fallen bottles by looking at the numbers printed on each one and counting the number of spots.

A number spinner

Collect together:

- A piece of 12cm by 12cm card.
- A pencil.
- Scissors.
- A ruler.

As an alternative to a dice (large dice can be obtained from good toy shops) you might like to make a number spinner.

To make the spinner

1 Draw a large hexagon on the piece of card and cut it out.
2 With the pencil and ruler divide the hexagon into eight equal sections and print the numbers 1 to 8 in each space. If you are teaching your child the written name for numbers you could use printed words.
3 Push a sharp pointed pencil through the centre of the hexagon.

To use the spinner

Stand the pencil up on its point and twist it sharply. The score is obtained by using the number which the spinner rests on when it stops spinning.

A car race game

(To make a game for two players.)

Collect together:

- 2 small toy cars.
- A sheet of card or paper, 45cm by 45cm. (Wall paper lining paper is ideal.)
- A thick felt tip pen.
- A large dice. (Obtainable from good toy shops.) Or a number spinner. (Instructions for making a spinner are included in this section.)

Make the game

On the sheet of paper draw a twisting race track. the track needs to be about 10cm wide, so that two small cars can fit side by side. With the pen, divide the track into roughly equal sections, about 8cm long.

Play the game

Put the cars side by side on the starting line. The first player spins the spinner or throws the dice and moves his car according to the number shown, e.g. if you throw a 3 you move three spaces. The winner is the one who reaches the finishing line first.

A number posting box

Number boxes

Collect together:

- *10 strong envelopes.*
- *An empty cardboard grocery box.*
- *A felt tip pen.*
- *10 pieces of card. These need to be small enough to fit into the envelopes.*
- *Sellotape.*
- *Felt tip pens or crayons.*

Make the game

1 Attach the envelopes around the outside of the cardboard box by sticking the envelope flaps on to the box with sellotape. You should still be able to put the cards into the envelopes.
2 On the front of each envelope write a number. I would suggest using the numbers 1 to 5 initially and at a later stage you could increase the range of numbers.
3 Draw number pictures on the cards, e.g. 1 dog, 2 cats, 3 hens, etc. Your child may well enjoy helping you to draw these pictures and colour them.

Play the game

Ask the child to put the number pictures into the correct envelopes.

Collect together:

- *10 empty shoe boxes. Most shoe shops are happy to give these away.*
- *10 sheets of paper, 10cm by 10cm.*
- *Sellotape.*
- *A felt tip pen.*

Make the game

1 Remove and discard the shoe box lids. Sellotape a piece of paper on to the end of each box.
2 Number the boxes 1 to 10, by printing a large number on to the paper-covered end of each box.
3 Stand the boxes in a row with all the numbers next to each other and in the right order.

Play the game

Ask the child to fill the boxes for you with the correct number of objects for each box. The objects must also be the same in each box, e.g. Box "1" = 1 toy farm animal. Box "2" = 2 spoons. Box "3" = 3 toy cars, etc. Obviously, to begin with you will need to help the child. After a couple of days, empty the boxes and start again with different objects.

Many children have a number frieze on their bedroom wall. These often have a number with a picture of an object or objects underneath. The Number boxes serve the same purpose but they are much more fun because they involve the child. She gathers and counts her own objects and she soon realises that all sorts of things can be grouped together and, unlike the pictures on a frieze, the objects can vary from day to day.

Individual buns

Cooking is an excellent activity as it provides plenty of opportunity for counting and demonstrates to the child the practical application of number.

Collect together:

- *A mixing bowl.*
- *A tablespoon.*
- *A teaspoon.*
- *Paper cake cases.*
- *A baking tray.*
- *Self-raising flour.*
- *Soft margarine.*
- *Sugar.*
- *Sultanas or currants.*
- *Milk/egg mixture. (1 egg to half a pint of milk)*

To make the cakes

1 Heat the oven to gas no. 6 or 180 degrees.
2 Your child should then measure out:

　1 heaped tablespoon of SR flour
　1 teaspoon of margarine
　2 teaspoons of sugar
　3 teaspoons of sultanas
　2 tablespoons of milk/egg mixture

The ingredients should be placed all together in the bowl and mixed together well. Spoon the mixture into paper cake cases and cook for 10 to 15 minutes. (Of course an adult should put the cakes into the oven and take them out.)

A pet shop picture

Collect together:

- *Catalogues, leaflets, magazines and old unwanted books which contain pictures of family pets.*
- *Scissors.*
- *Glue and a glue brush.*
- *A thick felt tip pen.*
- *A large sheet of paper.*

Play the game

Using the felt tip pen, divide the large sheet of paper into sections. Tell the child that each section is a cage in a pet shop and then ask her to look through the magazines etc. and to cut out as many pictures of pets as she can find. Sort the cut out pictures into groups, e.g. dogs, cats, mice, fish . . .

Assign each set of animals to a cage in the pet shop and stick the pets into position. When the last animal has been stuck into its appropriate cage or run, count the animals and see how many dogs, cats, and mice you have. Write the number clearly in the corner of each cage. This makes a particularly attractive picture for a child's bedroom wall.

All in a row

(To make a game for two players.)

Collect together:

- *20 small pieces of 5cm by 5cm card.*
- *A felt tip pen.*

Make the game

Write the numbers 1 to 10 on the pieces of card.
Each number should be on two cards.

Play the game

Each player is given a card with the number 1 on it.
The rest of the cards are spread out face downwards
between the two players. Each player takes a turn
at lifting a card.

If it is the next card in the row (i.e. number 2 comes
after number 1), he keeps the card and places it in
position next to his existing cards. If it isn't a card
he needs he places it face downwards on the
table. The winner is the one to complete the 1 to 10
row first.

..Five..

Size

Grading and sorting

Collect together:

A collection of objects of various sizes. The following list gives an idea of some of the possibilities . . .

- *Stones from the beach or garden.*
- *Shells.*
- *Socks of all sizes.*
- *Flowers, anything from a daisy to a sunflower.*
- *Toy bricks.*
- *Soft toys – children invariably have quite a collection of teddies etc.*

Play the game

Give the child the collection of objects e.g. soft toys, and ask her to find the biggest and the smallest toy. Having found these ask the child to go on to sort out the rest of the toys, putting them in a line in order of size.

Matching lids

Collect together:

- *10 variously sized lids from jars and bottles.*
- *A few sheets of coloured sticky-backed paper.*
- *A large sheet of paper or card. The size rather depends upon the size of the lids.*
- *A pencil.*
- *Scissors.*

Make the game

1 Draw round each lid or bottle top on the sticky coloured paper to make a set of outline shapes.
2 Cut the shapes out and stick them on to the larger sheet of paper in order of size.

Play the game

Give the child the collection of lids and the sheet of coloured shapes. Ask her to match each of the lids and tops with the same-sized coloured shape.

Family handprints

Collect together:

- *A bowl of handprint paint. To make the paint you simply mix together wallpaper paste (without fungicide) and dry powder paint or food colouring. The mixture needs to resemble thick cream.*
- *A large sheet of paper.*
- *Several smaller sheets of paper.*
- *Scissors.*
- *Glue and a glue brush.*

Play the game

Ask each member of the household to dip their hands in the handprint paint and to make a handprint on one of the smaller pieces of paper. Even the tolerant family dog can be included in this activity.

When all the prints are dry, cut them out and arrange them in order of size on the large sheet of paper. When your child is satisfied that the prints are in the correct order she can glue them into position.

Fill the egg cup

Collect together:

- *An egg cup.*

Play the game

Give your child the egg cup and ask him to fill it with as many different items as he can find, e.g. a grain of rice, a daisy, a paper clip, etc. The child will soon discover which objects are of an appropriate size.

If two or more children are playing this game they could have a little competition to see who can find the highest number of items.

A shoe shop

Collect together:

- *As many different shoes, boots and slippers as possible.*
- *A toy till or empty box.*
- *A handful of real money or clean milk bottle tops.*
- *Small squares of card with various prices written on them. It is best not to go above 10p.*

Play the game

Help the child to prepare his pretend shoe shop. Explain that the shoes will need to be arranged in order of size, i.e. daddy's large shoes at one end of the counter and baby's boots at the other. Place the price tags in position and play shop.

Children love to try on their parents' shoes so this game has an added attraction.

The Goldilocks game

(To make a game for two players)

Collect together:

- *2 large sheets of card, 30cm by 20cm.*
- *24 small pieces of card – each one should be 5cm by 10cm.*
- *A few extra pieces of card for making templates.*
- *A ruler.*
- *A felt tip pen.*

Make the game

1 With the felt tip pen and ruler divide the large sheets of card into 12 equal sections. Each section should be 10cm by 5cm.
2 In the top three sections on each card draw 3 simple bear shapes, one bear to each section – one large, one medium and one small. (Templates will help you to keep the shapes a regular size.)
3 In the next three sections (underneath the appropriate bear), draw 1 large bowl, 1 medium bowl and one small bowl. Beneath these draw 3 chairs and finally in the bottom three sections draw the three bears' beds.
4 The bears, bowls, chairs and beds should also be drawn on to the individual pieces of card. Again templates will help accuracy. When you have finished doing this you should have two small cards with large bears on, two with medium sized bears on, two with small bears and so on.

Play the game

Each player takes a large card.

Lay the small cards face downwards on the table top.

The players take turns at lifting a card and if it matches a picture on the large card, they place the small card on top of the picture. If they do not need the small card they return it face downwards on the table. The winner is the first one to cover the large card completely.

Mixed-up lids

Collect together:

- *A collection of clean, empty jars, bottles and boxes, with lids.*

Play the game

Take the lids off all the bottles, jars and boxes. Mix the lids up and give them to your child. Ask her to put the lids back on to the appropriate jars etc.

To start with it might be best to limit the number of containers and lids you give to the child but as she becomes more proficient the number can be increased.

Please remember that when playing with glass containers young children should be carefully supervised.

Dogs and bones

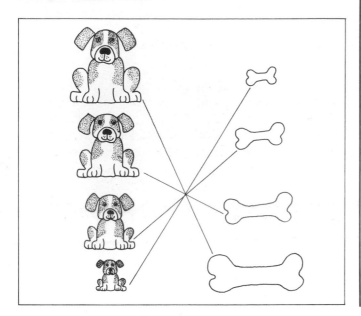

Collect together:

- *A sheet of paper.*
- *A pencil.*

Make the game

Draw a row of variously sized dogs down the left hand side of the paper and opposite the dogs draw a row of appropriately sized bones, i.e. a large bone for a large dog. The bones should not be in the correct order.

Play the game

Ask the child to draw a line from each dog to a bone. The largest dog should have the largest bone. You could extend this idea and draw teddy bears with pots of honey, spaceships with moons, hens with eggs, or indeed any suitable combination of pairs.

Colour

Egg box tiddly winks

Collect together:

- *2 empty egg boxes.*
- *Different coloured paints.*
- *Tiddly winks.*
- *Scissors.*
- *A felt tip pen.*

Make the game

1 Cut the lids from the egg boxes and paint inside the egg cups with different coloured paints. Paint two cups red, two blue and so on.
2 When the egg boxes have dried, stand them side by side.

Play the game

Decide on a colour score system, i.e. red cups score 1 point, blue cups score 2 points, etc. (You could always write the score with a felt tip pen in the bottom of each cup.)

Flick the tiddly winks into the cups from a short distance away or if this is too difficult for little ones simply throw the counters into the cups. The winner is the one with the highest score.

A colour collage

Collect together:

- *Old colourful magazines.*
- *Scissors.*
- *Glue and a glue brush.*
- *Scraps of material, wool and wrapping paper of the chosen colour.*
- *A sheet of paper.*

To make the collage

1 Help the child to decide on a colour, e.g. blue.
2 Look through the old magazines and find pictures of blue things, such as a blue dress and a blue car. The child should cut out as many blue pictures as possible and stick them, along with any scraps of blue material, wool and paper he might have, on to the sheet of paper.

A colour table

Decide on a colour, for example green.

Together with your child look around your home and make a collection of green objects. This could include green apples, a green jumper, a green toy car, a green pencil and so on.

Create a "green" table where the objects can be displayed. Your child can add to the green collection over a period of a few days. After a week start again with a new colour. This is an ideal way for little ones to learn their colours.

A colour scrap book

Collect together:

- *A scrap book you have made or bought.*
- *Scissors.*
- *Glue and a glue brush.*
- *Old magazines, comics, Christmas cards and pretty wrapping paper.*

Play the game

Each page of the scrap book should be devoted to a particular colour, e.g. The first page could be a "red" page, the next one "blue" and so on.

Look through the collection of magazines, cards, etc. and ask your child to cut out anything which has an obvious colour. The pictures can then be stuck on to the appropriate pages in the scrap book.

Lollipops lotto

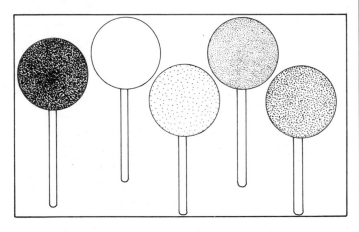

(To make a game for two players.)

Collect together:

- *2 pieces of card, 25cm by 20cm.*
- *Coloured felt tip pens.*
- *10 circles of card. Make these by drawing round a 10p coin.*
- *A 10p coin.*

Make the game

1 Draw 5 lollipops on each piece of card. Make the lollipop tops by drawing round the 10p coin.
2 Colour the lollipops with a variety of different colours.
3 Colour the circles of card in the same colours as you have used on the lollipops, i.e. one circle for each lollipop.

Play the game

Put the circles, colour side down on the table. The two players take turns to pick up a circle and name the colour on it. If it is the same colour as a lollipop on their card, they can cover the lollipop with the circle. A lollipop can only be covered once.

The winner is the one who covers all 5 lollipops first.

Colour sorting

Give your child a group of variously coloured objects, e.g. toy bricks, toy cars, Smarties, cotton reels. Ask her to sort them out for you by putting the same colours together. Talk about the colours as she does so, e.g. "That's a nice yellow Smartie. Are there any more? Are you wearing anything yellow?"

You should try to refer to different colours by name as often as possible.

Colour I-spy

Using the colours instead of the initial letter sounds of objects makes the traditional game of I-spy a much simpler game and one which can be enjoyed by very small children, e.g.

I spy with my little eye something which is white.

Take turns at playing the game and don't forget to pick out and use the more unfamiliar colours, such as grey, purple and silver.

Shapes

Shape pictures

Collect together:

- *Old colourful magazines.*
- *Scissors.*
- *Glue and a glue brush.*
- *A sheet of paper.*

Play the game

Together with your child, decide on a simple shape like a square or a circle. Look through the old magazines and see if you can find your shape in any of the pictures. For example, pictures of clocks and wheels are circles.

Cut out as many of the chosen shapes as you can find and stick them on to the paper.

A solids table

It is difficult for very young children to think in terms of three dimensions. They often call a sphere (i.e. a ball) a circle, or a cube (i.e. a play brick) a square. A table entirely devoted to the display of a particular solid shape can help them to understand, feel and see the difference between two dimensional and three dimensional objects.

For example, if you decide that your table is going to be devoted to "cylinders", you can ask your child to help you collect together some tin cans, the centre from a toilet roll, a rolling pin, a tumbler and so on. Place the collection on a convenient table or window ledge and put a label with the word "cylinders" next to the display. After a few days start again with a different solid shape, e.g. cubes.

Robbie the robot

Collect together:

- *2 sheets of card, 20cm by 20cm.*
- *Scissors.*
- *A pencil.*
- *A ruler.*
- *A few sheets of coloured sticky-backed paper.*
- *A felt tip pen.*

Make the game

1 Draw some different shapes on to the sticky-backed paper. These might include circles, rectangles, squares and triangles. You could also make each shape in two different sizes.
2 Cut the shapes out and stick them on to one of the sheets of card. Then cut the shapes out for a second time. You should now have a collection of colourful, card-backed shapes.
3 Draw a large square on the second sheet of card.

Play the game

Ask the child to make a robot's face by arranging the shapes on the large square. He could for instance use two triangles for eyes, a square for a nose and a rectangle for a mouth.

When the child has completed one face he can use the shapes again to create a completely different face. Do remember to name the shapes as the child plays with them.

Shapes lotto

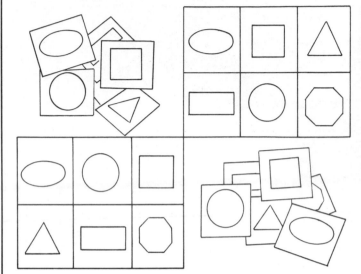

(To make a game for two players)

Collect together:

- *2 large sheets of 30cm by 20cm card.*
- *12 pieces of 9cm by 9cm card.*
- *A ruler.*
- *A felt tip pen.*

Make the game

1 Divide the two large sheets of card into six equal sections. Each section should be 10cm by 10cm.
2 In each section draw a shape, i.e. a triangle, a square, a circle, a rectangle, an oval and a hexagon.
3 On the twelve small cards draw the shapes again. (Draw each shape twice.)

Play the game

Each player takes a large card. The small cards are spread picture side down between the players. Each player takes a turn at lifting a small card and, if she can, she uses it to cover an identical shape on her card. You could also add the rule that all shapes must be named before they are covered.

The winner is the first one to cover all her shapes.

Make a house

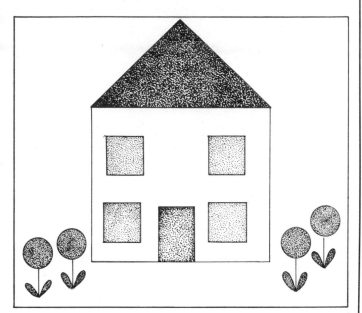

(To make a game for two players)

Collect together:

- *4 sheets of 25cm by 25cm card.*
- *A ruler.*
- *A pencil.*
- *A felt tip pen.*
- *Scissors.*
- *Crayons.*
- *A dice or number spinner.*

Make the game

1 On two of the sheets of card draw an identical simple house. Include the following shapes in the design: "square" windows, a "rectangular" door, a "triangular" roof, and some "circle" flowers in the garden.
2 Use the second two pieces of card to cut out a set of the shapes you have used on the houses.

Make sure that the cut-out shapes are exactly the same size as the house shapes. Colour the cut-outs, using a separate colour for each shape.
3 Each cut out shape is given a value, e.g. squares = 1, circles = 2, etc. It might help your child to remember the number if you print it on to the back of each shape.

Play the game

Each player is given a house card. The players take turns at throwing the dice and taking the cut-out shapes whose numbers correspond to the thrown numbers. The player places the cut out on top of the same shape on his card. If the dice shows an unwanted number, e.g. a 6, the player misses a turn.

The winner is the first one to cover his house with cut out shapes.

Shape stickers

Collect together:

- *Colourful paper cut into various shapes.*
- *Blu-Tack.*

Play the game

Take the shapes and the Blu-Tack and together with your child go for a walk around the house. Whenever you see an appropriately shaped object ask the child to stick a shape sticker on to it, e.g. a clock face could have a circle sticker placed on it and a bathroom tile a square sticker. Each time your child uses a sticker remind them of the name of the shape.

After a few days the child could be asked to "hunt" down all the shape stickers and bring them back to you. It is best to "hunt" one shape at a time.

Time

A time diary

Collect together:

- *An artist's plain paper sketch pad or some plain white paper stapled together.*
- *A felt tip pen.*
- *A jam jar lid to draw round.*
- *Crayons.*

Make the diary

On the top left hand corner of each page, draw round the jam jar lid and print a clock face without hands.

How to use the diary

Talk to the child about her day. What time does she get up in the morning? (Pick the nearest hour. Don't bother to introduce half hours or minutes at this stage.) If the answer is 7.00, let the child watch while you draw the hands on the first clock in the diary to show 7.00. Ask the child to draw a picture of herself getting up at seven underneath the clock.

Throughout the rest of the day make entries in the time diary. I would suggest you include what your child is doing at 10.00, 12.00, 2.00, 5.00 and so on until bed time.

If your child is out for part of the day, shopping or at playgroup, she can fill in the time diary when she returns home.

A paper plate clock

Collect together:

- *A large paper plate.*
- *A brass paper fastener.*
- *Scissors.*
- *A felt tip pen.*
- *A ruler.*
- *A pencil.*
- *2 strips of 10cm by 2cm card.*

To make the clock

1 Draw a simple clock face, minus hands, on the front of the paper plate.
2 Cut out a long hand and a short hand from the pieces of card and attach the hands to the centre of the clock face with the brass paper fastener.

To use the clock

To begin with, talk about the numbers around the outside of the clock and then move on to show the position of the hands for simple times such as 1.00, 2.00 etc. At specific times during the day ask your child to put the hands in the right position on the clock, e.g. at 9.00 playgroup time, 12.00 lunchtime or 7.00 storytime.

A Coco the clown calendar

to the clown by pressing the fasteners through the clown's body. Do make sure that the arrows can move.

Play the game

Hang the clown picture on a convenient wall or door and ask the child to point each arrow towards the appropriate section. Repeat this at intervals through the week and through the year.

Using a timer

Collect together:

- *A large sheet of paper, 50cm by 30cm.*
- *3 small paper plates.*
- *3 strips of 5cm by 1cm card.*
- *3 brass paper fasteners.*
- *A felt tip pen.*
- *A pencil.*
- *A ruler.*
- *Crayons.*
- *Scissors.*

Make the game

1 Using the pencil and ruler divide the first paper plate into 7 and then use the felt tip pen to print out the names of the days of the week on the outside edge of each section. Divide the second plate into 4 sections and print out the names of the four seasons in each one and finally divide the last plate into 12 sections and print out the names of the months of the year.
2 On the large sheet of paper draw a large clown shape. Make sure his body is large enough to contain all three plates and then use the crayons to give him some colour. Your child will probably enjoy helping you to do this.
3 Use the scissors to cut the three 5cm by 1cm strips into arrow shapes.
4 Attach an arrow to the centre of each plate with a brass paper fastener and then attach the plates

Many cookers have a timer attached but if you can buy a mechanical egg timer you will find it a very useful piece of equipment for your child.

The timer can be used in a variety of ways to help your child learn how to estimate time, e.g. If your child is slow at getting dressed in the morning, ask him to beat the bell by dressing before it rings. Tell him how many minutes you are setting on the timer before he starts to dress. At other times he could try to complete a jigsaw before the bell rings, or drink a glass of milk. You could set it to ring at bedtime or when his favourite TV programme starts, and of course cooking his boiled egg for tea is greatly assisted by the use of the timer.

Each time it is used, carefully explain how many minutes are involved. In this way your child should learn what "in a minute" really means and he will build up some understanding of the length of time.

A seasons collage

Collect together:

- *A long strip of paper. (Wallpaper lining paper is ideal.)*
- *Glue and a glue brush.*
- *A felt tip pen.*
- *Together with your child make a collection of suitably seasonal pictures and objects, e.g.*

Winter
A holly leaf, cotton wool, old Christmas cards, silver glitter, tin foil and shiny red paper.

Spring
Yellow and pink tissue paper, pictures of spring flowers and baby animals, old Easter cards, pieces of ribbon, shiny green paper and crushed egg shells.

Summer
Small shells or pasta shells, sand, old postcards, old bus and train tickets, pictures of ice-cream and fizzy drinks, gold paper.

Autumn
Orange and brown tissue paper leaves, twigs, pictures of bonfires and fireworks (the child could draw these herself), pictures of apples and other fruits.

To make the collage

Use the felt tip pen to divide the strip of paper into 4 equal sections and at the top of each section write the name of one of the four seasons.

Provide the child with one set of the seasonal objects at a time and ask her to stick these into the appropriate section. Talk about the different seasons as she works. The topics could include the weather, the clothes you wear, the food you might eat etc.

Measurement

Measuring with your body

Here is a question you might ask your child.

"I wonder how many strides you take when you walk down the hall? Let's count them and see."

After counting her strides along the hall, why not count how many she takes to cross the living room? Which took the most strides, hall or living room?

In this activity and in answering your questions, your child is discovering something of simple measurement. Indeed long before formal measuring devices were introduced, people used their bodies to measure in much the same way.

You don't have to restrict yourself to strides. Any part of the child's body could be used. e.g. "Let's see how many thumbs we can fit along this book?"

You needn't confine yourself to inside the house either. Count the number of strides between lamp posts on the way to the shops.

How tall is teddy?

Collect together:

- *5 or 6 pieces of 20cm by 20cm card.*
- *A collection of identical small objects, e.g. paper clips or small bricks.*
- *A felt tip pen.*

Make the game

Draw an outline shape of an animal or toy on each of the pieces of card. Make sure that the picture starts at the bottom of each card, i.e. teddy's feet should be right on the bottom edge.

Play the game

Give the child the collection of small items, e.g. small bricks, and one of the cards. Starting at the bottom of the card, the bricks are placed next to each other in a line until the top of the picture is reached. How many bricks did it take to reach the top of teddy?

How tall am I?

Collect together:

- *A long strip of card, approx 30cm wide and at least 150cm long.*
- *A ruler.*
- *A felt tip pen.*
- *Crayons.*
- *Blu-Tack.*

Make the game

1 Draw a line down the centre of the strip and mark it in centimetres. For the first metre it is only really necessary to mark every 10cm.
2 Decorate the strip with pictures. It is always fun to reflect on the changes in your child as he grows and so the pictures at the bottom of the strip could feature baby toys and as you move up the strip you can include his current interests and pastimes. Your child will obviously love to help you to do this.
3 Stick the strip to the wall with Blu-Tack.

Play the game

Every few months ask your child to take his shoes off and stand against the strip. Record his height by drawing an arrow next to the cm mark and write down the date.

Children love to see themselves growing and just to see the marks on the chart moving upwards is very exciting for them.

Using scales

Collect together:

- *Traditional kitchen scales. The type with two pans.*
- *A collection of small objects, e.g. acorns, conkers, toy farm animals, a paper bag full of cotton wool, toy bricks, etc.*

To use the scales

Show the child how to balance the scales and then set him some simple questions, e.g. Which is heavier the bag of cotton wool or the brick? How many conkers do you need to balance the toy car?

Of course children also love to help to use the scales during cooking activities and when time permits they should be allowed to measure out the ingredients.

Using string as a measure

Collect together:

- *A ball of string.*
- *Scissors.*
- *Paper.*
- *A pencil.*
- *Sellotape.*

Play the game

To start with, use the ball of string to measure different parts of your child's body. For example, when measuring his head, wrap the string around the top of the head and carefully cut the string where it meets together. You could also measure his wrist, ankle, finger, arm, waist and chest. To make identifying the strings easier you can mark each one with a label made from the paper and Sellotape.

When you have finished measuring, lay all the strings side by side so that the child can see for himself which is the longest and shortest. You can later move on to measuring other members of the family and comparing their sizes.

String can also be used to measure toys, books, shoes, bananas, forks, the letter box and indeed absolutely anything. At this stage there is no need to mention centimetres.

Money

A pocket money chart

	Monday	Tuesday	Wednesday	Thursday	Friday	Saturday	Sunday
2p	✓			✓	✓		
3p		✓			✓		✓
5p	✓						✓
5p			✓		✓		
10p				✓			

Collect together:

- *A small piece of paper.*
- *A large sheet of paper.*
- *A ruler.*
- *A felt tip pen.*

To make the chart

1 On the small piece of paper make a list of all the little jobs that your child can do and give each job a payment price, e.g.

Putting the milk bottles out for the milkman = 2p
Feeding the dog = 3p
Tidying her bedroom = 5p

2 Divide the large sheet of paper into squares. You will need 8 squares across and as many squares down as you have jobs.
3 Missing out the first square on the top left hand side, write out the days of the week along the top of the paper.
4 Down the left hand side of the paper write out the jobs your child could do, plus the price for each one. It is also a good idea to draw a small picture of each job, e.g. a picture of a bed for tidying the bedroom.
5 Pin the chart to a convenient wall or door.

To use the chart

Each time your child completes a job she ticks the appropriate square and writes the payment price next to the tick. At the end of the week the amounts are added up and the payment is made.

Coin rubbing

Collect together:

- *Sheets of paper.*
- *Black wax crayons or a thick black pencil.*
- *A handful of coins.*

To play the game

Give the child the coins and ask her to put them one at a time underneath the sheet of paper and then to gently rub over the top of the coin with the black crayon. The patterns and pictures on the coin will emerge through the paper.

This is a useful activity as it helps the child to recognise the different coins and if they are then cut out and mounted on card they can be used as pretend money for a pretend shop.

A pretend shop

The benefits of having a pretend shop for your child are enormous. A few tins and packets from the cupboard along with some fruit and vegetables, a toy till or a shoe box of money (real money or clean milk bottle tops), and a handful of simple price tickets, (nothing over 10p) provide the basis for imaginative play with a lot of learning potential.

Ask the child to arrange the stock in the shop, this will automatically involve the child in "sorting" out the fruit and the different types of tins and packets. The price tickets can then be put on the groceries.

When buying or selling, the child will be actively involved in simple counting, recognising numbers and coins, taking away, and division. Ideally you should be around to provide the language he needs to understand the concepts he is dealing with. Simple questions from you such as "How many milk bottle tops have you got left? Have you got enough to buy this orange? Let's count these apples and see if we can all have one each", will help your child to think about the numbers and amounts involved.

Older children could even be encouraged to keep a stock book and count the takings at the end of a session.

Fill the purse

(To make a game for two players.)

Collect together:

- *2 sheets of 20cm by 20cm card.*
- *A felt tip pen.*
- *Some real money.*
- *A money spinner. Detailed instructions on how to make a spinner can be found in the Number section, but instead of the usual numbers divide the spinner into six sections and print out the amounts, 50p, 20p, 10p, 5p, 2p, and 1p.*

Make the game

1 Draw a simple purse shape on each of the sheets of card.
2 Inside each purse draw the outline shape of two 50p's, two 10p's, two 20p's, two 5p's, two 2p's and three 1p's. The simplest method of doing this is to draw round the coins themselves.
3 Print the value of each coin inside each shape.

Play the game

Each player takes a purse card. Taking turns, the players spin the money spinner and pick up the appropriate coin. The coins are used to cover the coin shapes in the purse. The first one to fill his purse with real money is the winner.

Coin sorting

Collect together:

- *6 saucers.*
- *Loose change containing 50p's, 20p's, 10p's, 5p's, 2p's and 1p's.*

Play the game

In the bottom of each saucer put a different coin, e.g. saucer 1 would contain a 1p, saucer 2 would contain a 2p, etc.

Give the child the loose change and ask her to sort it out for you by putting the coins in the correct saucers.